DEAD END FEMINISM

Elisabeth Badinter

Translated by Julia Borossa

polity

First published in French as *Fausse route* by Elisabeth Badinter
© Odile Jacob, April 2003

This translation first published in 2006 © Polity Press

This work is published with the assistance of the French Ministry of
Culture – National Centre for the Book.
Ouvrage publié avec le concours du Ministère français chargé de la
culture – Centre national du livre.

This book is supported by the French Ministry for Foreign Affairs, as
part of the Burgess programme headed for the French Embassy in
London by the Institut Français du Royaume Uni.

ⅱ institut français

Polity Press
65 Bridge Street
Cambridge CB2 1UR, UK

Polity Press
350 Main Street
Malden, MA 02148, USA

ISBN: 0-7456-3380-3
ISBN: 0-7456-3381-1 (pb)

A catalogue record for this book is available from the British Library.

Typeset in 11 on 13 pt Berling
by Servis Filmsetting Ltd, Manchester
Printed and bound in India by
Replika Press Pvt. Ltd

For further information on Polity, visit our website: www.polity.co.uk

L
26.4.01

Dead End Feminism

For my daughter Judith

Contents

The Turning Point of the 1990s

It takes a huge effort of memory to recall the spirit of the 1980s. After the great victories of the previous decade and the rise of the left in power in France, every kind of hope was allowed. For some women it was a time for enthusiasm, even euphoria. Feminists could take pleasure in the glorious results that had been achieved in less then twenty years. The massive growth of women's presence in the workforce was finally making independence possible. Once a woman can support herself and her children, she can leave a man she can no longer stand. This came as a precious freedom, almost unknown to the previous generation. Divorce was on the increase, and traditional marriage gradually lost its meaning. Goodbye to these age-old shackles! With contraception and abortion, Western women found themselves holding a degree of power unprecedented in the history of humanity. Like it or not, this revolution meant the end of patriarchy. Men were told: 'you will be a father if I want, when I want.' And finally, the names of those who forged ahead for the first time into areas that had previously been exclusively male were recited as so many victories. From the first woman accepted at the Ecole Polytechnique, to the first female president of the Family Court, via the first female police commissioner and many other 'firsts', the general feeling was of a profound upheaval taking place in the ways in which gender was being defined. _even in theatre women_

The image of the traditional woman was being effaced, to be replaced by another one: a more virile, stronger woman, almost in control of herself, if not of the universe. At long last the roles were changing! After millennia of a more or less gentle tyranny that had relegated her to supporting roles, woman was finally to become the heroine of the movie, while men would only be extras. Such a pleasurable reversal was certainly the source of a precious energy for women pushing out towards new limits. In fact, there were no more limits. All that was his belonged to her, but all that was hers did not belong to him. Full of this conquering spirit, women saw themselves as soon to share the world as well as the home with their male companions. The equality of the sexes was perceived as the ultimate measure of a true democracy.

Unaffected by the new wave of American feminism which was developing an essentialist, separatist and 'nationalist' discourse, recreating a new oppositional sexual dualism, French women dreamed of an easier relationship with the men in their lives: father, husband, boss and all the others.

Only academic feminists had read or heard about the fury of the talented Andrea Dworkin or the battles the legal expert Catharine MacKinnon was waging against sexual harassment and pornography. In the mid-1980s, American feminists were already denouncing every kind of violence against women, and so fostering an ever increasing mistrust of the male sex, while on the other side of the Atlantic it was the double working day and the inexplicable inertia of men that preoccupied women. It is true that French society was less brutal then than it is now, and that the victims of male violence did not often make themselves known. So it was not so much the enforcement of the 1980 legislation against rape, as the success of a humorous and unacrimonious little book, Michèle Fitoussi's *Le ras-le-bol des superwomen* [Superwomen are fed up], that marked a change in sensibilities. Published in 1987, it was a book by a thirty-two year old journalist, a mother of two. It was the first stone thrown into the garden of 1970s feminism and it landed with a great thud. The title itself became an expression readily used in the press. The *ras-le-bol* became a new way of saying 'we've been had'.

Since a return to the previous state of things could not be envisaged, and there was no question of sacrificing either their family or their professional life, most women felt obliged, whatever the cost, to continue along the path marked out by their mothers. However, the time of cheerful marches towards victory had passed. Instead, a psychological journey remained to be taken, one fusing with a new social sensibility. This included women's disappointment in men. Most men have not played their part in the game of equality. Or anyway, have not played it well enough or fast enough. The comparative timetables of men and women who have children make this clear. Nothing has really changed in the last twenty years: women continue to be responsible for three-quarters of all family and household tasks. It is more than enough to make you bitter ... And naturally, disappointment turns into resentment. Resentment against feminists who, after having trumpeted unrealizable objectives, then took refuge in either silence or *mea culpa*. Resentment against the state, controlled by men, and which doesn't give a damn about the problems mothers face. Finally, resentment against men, who, not content with resisting their companions with the force of boundless inertia, also engage in hand-to-hand combat to preserve their private domain: the corridors of power.

This sad state of affairs became magnified at the beginning of the 1990s by the rigours of an economic crisis that had been simmering for more than fifteen years. Millions of men, and proportionally even more women, experienced unemployment. The time was no longer favourable to feminist demands. On the contrary, society folded in on itself and many mothers of two children, especially those who were economically the weakest, returned to the home, in exchange for half of the minimum wage.

At the same time as this experience of powerlessness was occurring, a new sensibility gradually emerged in society, causing a reversal of our hierarchy of values. From the end of the 1980s, and even more so today, the Western world has surrendered with pleasure to what Pascal Bruckner has called the *temptation of innocence*. The new heroic figure is no longer the warrior who lifts mountains, it is the defenceless victim. 'Misfortune is the equivalent of being chosen, it ennobles the one who experiences it, and to claim it means setting oneself apart from common humanity, turning failure into glory [. . .] I suffer therefore I am worthy,' concludes Bruckner. Any kind of suffering calls for denunciation and reparation. The general cult of victimhood in society has meant a prolife-ration of tribunals. There is talk only of penalties and sanc-tions.

Feminism has not escaped this process. On the contrary, it has been one of its main champions. High-achieving women are less interesting than the victims of male domination. Superwoman has a bad press. At best, she is the exception to the rule, at worst an egoistical privileged person who has broken the pact of solidarity with her suffering sisters. Nothing has been more revealing than the way women's magazines have treated the unprecedented achievement of the yachtswoman Ellen MacArthur. The fact that this slip of a woman has won one of the most epic Route du Rhum races, leaving behind the most seasoned sailors, has given rise to only lukewarm enthusiasm. Admittedly *Elle* had as its cover story 'Notre heroine' [Our heroine], but did not deem it nec-essary to have her appear on the cover, as had been the case with Florence Arthaud a few years earlier. And *Madame Figaro* devoted only a few sentences to Ellen MacArthur as a caption to a photograph, taking care to divide up the compli-ments between her and one of her unfortunate rivals, who had 'the courage to confess his fear and turned back a few hours after setting off'.

The exploits of sportswomen, especially when they leave behind their male colleagues, are less anecdotal than it would seem. They demonstrate courage and will-power. They break with the image of the powerless woman, the woman who needs protection, so dear to American radicals. High calibre sportswomen, great journalists, or any other women who forge ahead into male territory disturb the dominant ideology. So it is preferable to ignore them and to concentrate attention on the theme of eternal male oppression.

Nothing has changed, according to some. Things are now worse, according to others. Never before has male violence been so obviously laid out for dissection. Social violence and sexual violence are one and the same thing. A finger is pointed at the guilty one: it is man in all his guises. Many sociologists and anthropologists keep trotting out the same desperate observation: whether a product of nature or of culture, male supremacy is universal. Without forgetting its corollary: women are always and everywhere in a position of subordination, in other words they are real or potential victims. It is rarely admitted that this unfortunate situation no longer holds true in the domain of reproduction . . . And when it is admitted, not all the consequences are drawn.[1]

This 'victim'[2] perspective is not without its advantages. First of all, you immediately feel you are on the right side of the barricades. Not only because the victim is always right, but because she elicits a sympathy that is proportional to the merciless hatred that is felt towards her tormentor. Penal experts are well aware of this: the public rarely identifies with the criminal in the dock. In addition, the victimization of the female gender allows for the condition of women and feminist discourse to be united under a common banner. Thus the conundrum of cultural, social or economic differences vanishes at the stroke of a magic wand. We can compare without blushing the condition of 'European' and 'Oriental' women and affirm that 'everywhere, women, because they are women, are victims of hatred and violence'.[3] The bourgeois lady of the seventh arrondissement and the young *beurette* [Arab girl][4] from the suburbs: it's all the same fight.

However, by conflating real and false victims, we risk misunderstanding the urgency of the battles to be waged. To endlessly emphasize the image of woman as defenceless and oppressed in the face of her hereditary oppressor means losing all credibility with the younger generation, which does not see it this way. In fact, what are they being offered, other than evermore victimhood and penalties? Nothing to get excited about. Nothing that could change their day-to-day life, either. On the contrary, obsessed by putting the male sex on trial, and by identity issues, the feminism of these last few years has left behind the very battles that have been its raison d'être. Sexual freedom gives way to the ideal of a domesticated sexuality, while the myth of the maternal instinct reappears without anybody raising an eyebrow. It is true that we have returned to the implicit definition of woman through motherhood in order to justify the inscription of sexual difference in the Constitution, as if having more women in legislative assemblies was worth letting the old stereotypes take pride of place once again.

We have to ask ourselves these questions now: What real progress has been achieved in the last fifteen years? Does the feminist discourse in the media today[5] correctly reflect the preoccupations of the majority of women? What paradigms of masculinity and femininity does it try to promote? What models of sexuality does it seek to impose? So many questions that sometimes call for a detour via the United States. Not because we have bought the Americans' merchandise wholesale. But because, with some delay, as usual, we have taken some of their ideas and mixed them up with ours. The results remain to be judged.

1
The New Discourse on Method

The Cartesian criteria of truth have long lost their currency. In place of 'clear and distinct' ideas we prefer analogy and generalization. In short, we prefer the amalgam which consists in 'combining diverse elements that hardly go together'.[1] The amalgam is less the instrument of the scholar than of the politician. In fact, the philosophy that founds the current victim feminism is difficult to pin down. It concerns different vague conceptualizations where culturalism rubs shoulders with naturalism and an essentialism that never speaks its name. It often gives the impression that principles do not rule actions but rather that actions produce justifications after the fact. What is at stake is not so much a theory of the relationship between the sexes as the trial of the other sex and of a system of oppression. It is a new logic, but an old philosophy. Whether it likes it or not, this feminism has given birth to a representation of woman that either runs the risk of turning back the clock considerably, or else of taking us where we do not want to go.

The logic of amalgamation

This logic of amalgamation is applied above all to the domain of sexuality and proceeds by generalizations and analogies.

We no longer distinguish between the objective and the subjective, the minor and the major, the normal and the pathological, the physical and the psychical, the conscious and the unconscious. In the name of a particular conception of sexuality and of the relationship between the sexes, everything is levelled out.

The continuum of violence

For the last thirty years, American radical feminism has patiently woven together the threads of a continuum of sex crimes that tries to demonstrate a long female martyrdom. In the space of a few years three books came out of this current, all putting to the fore the theme of the sexual oppression of women. The first addressed rape, the second, sexual harassment, and the last one, pornography. Their authors, Susan Brownmiller,[2] Catharine MacKinnon[3] and Andrea Dworkin,[4] derived a considerable celebrity status out of them. Afterwards, Dworkin and MacKinnon continued to work together, since they agreed on the essential: women are an oppressed class, and sexuality is the very root of that oppression. Male domination rests on the power that enables men to treat women as sexual objects. This power is seen as going back to the origins of the species, and is supposed to have been inaugurated by rape. Above all, in their eyes, rape, sexual harassment, pornography, and assault and battery make up a whole that reflects the same kind of violence against women.[5] And let us not forget prostitution, striptease and everything that touches on sexuality from near or afar. The verdict is without appeal: men must be forced to change their sexuality. And the means: modifying the law and using the tribunals.

Liberal feminists vehemently protested against such an approach that called for censorship, trampled on sexual freedom and sounded like a declaration of war against the male gender.[6] Doubling her provocations, Andrea Dworkin was left to her excesses and served as a foil for this new feminism. Her victim philosophy did, however, become quite influential. She did not hesitate to compare women to the survivors of concentration camps, and afterwards many other hands penned the word *survivor*. It is her accomplice MacKinnon, a brilliant lawyer and a law professor at prestigious universities, who led the legal battle with the success that we know. Not only was she instrumental in sexual harassment becoming recognized as a form of sexual discrimination by the United States Supreme Court in 1986, but allied to the most conservative lobbies and with the unfailing support of the Republican Party, she succeeded in having the ordinance that became known as the 'MacKinnon–Dworkin' ordinance against pornography voted through twice, in 1983 and in 1984, in the cities of Minneapolis and Indianapolis. Pornography having become a violation of civil rights, the ordinance could be applied indiscriminately to films, books or newspapers. From the moment that a woman said she felt in a 'state of subordination', she could undertake to have the cause of her humiliation prohibited. Entire sections of classical literature and cinema were in danger of getting the chop. This time feminists of all persuasions (from Betty Friedan to Kate Millett, via Adrienne Rich) were vocal in their opposition to this delirium of censorship. After a heated battle, the First Amendment on free speech was invoked against the ordinance. But MacKinnon's prestige expanded massively, and with it her audience. Even to the point that in 1992 the Canadian Supreme Court adopted a good part of her theories on pornography.

Strangely, neither Dworkin or MacKinnon had their books translated into French. Perhaps they were judged to be incompatible with the state of mind of French women. Even more strangely, their names rarely appear in feminist writings. It is as if their open extremism let off an overly sulphurous smell. However, a number of their ideas have crossed the Atlantic, via our friends from Quebec, European institutions and the many academics who frequent the American campuses where these ideas are preached the most.

In France, it all started with a healthy awakening. In 1978 an exemplary trial of three rapists in Aix-en-Provence was enlightening for the whole society. The trial was conducted

masterfully by the prosecutor Gisèle Halimi, the representative of the two victims and the president of the association
Choisir la Cause des Femmes [Choose the cause of women].[7]
It turned into a trial of rape itself, all too often assimilated to
simple indecent assault; a trial of the police and of a justice
system that discourages women from pressing charges by
adding humiliation to suspicion; a trial, finally, of a society
that does not recognize the seriousness of sex crimes, because
a 'world of male values has, in fact, justified rape by invoking
the "natural aggressive virility of men" and "the masochistic
passivity of women"'.[8] It is thanks to this exemplary trial that
it began to be said that psychological wounds took more time
to heal than physical ones. Hidden or unrecognized suffering
is irreversible. The Aix victims spoke of destruction, loss of
identity and death. As G. Vigarello correctly points out, 'the
reference to inner trauma [. . .] became one of the main reference points in assessing the severity of the crime.'[9]

Following the Aix trial, rape was redefined and requalified.
The law of 23 December 1980 stipulates: 'Any act of sexual
penetration, whatever its nature, committed against another
person by violence, constraint, threat or surprise is rape.'[10]
The penalties that can be incurred range from five to twenty
years in prison, depending on the circumstances of the crime.
Despite much resistance to taking legal action, rape charges
continued to increase: 892 in 1992; 1,238 in 1996.[11] The
most striking aspect is the increase in the sentences in the ten
to twenty years range: these rose from 283 in 1992 to 514 in
1996.[12] Apart from rape, other sexual offences would also
come to be redefined and requalified. The new penal code of
1992 no longer speaks of 'offences against public decency'
but of 'sexual aggression': 'sexual aggression is any sexual
assault committed with violence, constraint, threat or surprise.'[13] The notion of sexual assault is enlarged and 'a whole
new era of ostracized actions is introduced',[14] including
moral and psychological violence.

In 1992, following the American example, the new offence
of 'sexual harassment' was created, complementing the
older charge of abuse of power. Thanks to the wisdom of

Parliament and of Véronique Neiertz, Minister
Rights at that time, the text that was adopted lii
ties to cases involving hierarchical relations. Ir
Americans who were surprised by such a limitatic
ister apparently replied that she would advise w̲.̲.̲.̲c̲ı̲ı̲ who
felt harassed by their work colleagues to respond by giving
them 'a good slap in the face'.[15] This demonstration of
common sense was soon forgotten. Ten years later, the law of
17 January 2002 introduced the new offence of moral harassment which eliminated the element of authority.[16] Sexual or
moral harassment by sleazy bosses is a phenomenon that is
well known in the workplace, and it was right to penalize it.
But for the rest, would it not have been better to encourage
women (and men) to defend themselves, rather than to consider them to be defenceless beings?

On 17 April 2002, Mme Anna Diamantopoulou,
Commissioner in charge of employment and social affairs,
announced that the European Parliament had just adopted a
legislation against sexual harassment, defined in the following way: 'An unwelcome form of verbal, non-verbal or physical behaviour of a sexual nature that undermines the dignity
of a person, by creating an intimidating, hostile, degrading,
humiliating or offensive situation.'[17] Not only could a
harasser be a colleague or a subordinate, but the terms in use
are so imprecise and so subjective that anything can qualify
as harassment. Contrary to the current French legislation, this
definition does not even include the notion of 'repeated acts'.
It leaves the door open to ideas such as *visual harassment* (an
overly insistent gaze) or other such nonsense. How then do
we distinguish between the objective and the subjective, the
real and the imaginary? Not to speak of the line that separ-
ates violence from sexual intent. As an undisputable example
of violence, Mme Diamantopoulou cites the displaying of
pornographic photographs on walls, hinting at her next
target. Without a doubt, we are witnessing an American type
of slippery slope. We are not far from the moment when
sexual harassment will be defined, as at Princeton, as 'any
undesired sexual attention that engenders a feeling of malaise

or that causes problems at school, at work or in social relations'.

Extending the concept of violence to verbal aggression and psychological pressure, as the recent survey Nommer et Compter les Violences envers les Femmes en France – Naming and counting acts of violence in relation to women in France (the Enveff study) – argues should be done,[18] leaves the door open to all kinds of possible interpretations. How does one measure in a closed questionnaire an 'attack on a person's psychic integrity'? Where does an insult in a public place begin and where does it end? One woman might experience it as such, but another might not. It is left to their personal judgement. The same is true for what might constitute psychological pressure in a relationship. Of the nine questions that are supposed to measure this type of violence (see box), there are some that leave one puzzled. This one, for instance: 'During the last 12 months, did your spouse or partner: Criticize, ridicule what you were doing? Make unpleasant remarks concerning your physical appearance? Impose certain clothes, hairstyles, or public behaviour? Not take your opinions into account, express contempt or try to tell you what to think?'[19] The sense of unease increases on finding that these psychological pressures – which receive the greatest number of affirmative answers – figure in the list of global indicators of domestic violence right next to 'verbal insults and threats' and 'emotional blackmail' and on the same level as 'physical aggression' and 'rape and other forced sexual acts' (see table 1 on p. 14). The global indicator for domestic violence calculated in such a way thus comes out as affecting 10 per cent of French women, taking account of the fact that 37 per cent of them complain of psychological pressure, 2.5 per cent of physical aggression and 0.9 per cent of rape or other forced sexual acts.

Puzzlement reigns supreme. Is it possible to add physical acts to psychological feelings as if both were the same kind of thing? Is it legitimate to speak in the same breath of rape and of an unpleasant or wounding remark? It could be said that pain is experienced in both cases. But would it not be more

---

Excerpt from the questionnaire: Psychological pressure in the person's relationship with her partner

During the last 12 months, did your spouse or partner:
never/rarely/sometimes/often/regularly

1 prevent you from meeting or talking to friends or family members?
2 prevent you from talking to other men?
3 criticize, ridicule what you were doing?
4 make unpleasant remarks concerning your physical appearance?
5 impose certain clothes, hairstyles, or public behaviour?
6 not take your opinion into account, express contempt or try to tell you what to think (a) at home (b) in public?
7 insist on knowing where and with whom you were?
8 refuse to speak to you, refuse point-blank to discuss anything?
9 refuse access to household funds for daily expenses?

Source: ENVEFF survey 2000; *Population et sociétés*, no. 364 (Jan. 2001), p. 4.

---

rigorous to distinguish between objective and subjective pain, between violence, abuse of power and rudeness? The term violence is linked to such an extent in our minds to physical violence that we run the risk of creating a regrettable confusion and the impression that 10 per cent of French women suffer physical attacks from their partner.[20]

Adding up heterogeneous forms of violence in such a way while relying on the simple testimony of people contacted by telephone allows subjectivity to take centre stage. Without the partner being confronted and without in-depth interviews, how can results obtained in such a way be taken at face value?

The logic of amalgamation does not end there. Perhaps due to the common root of words such as *viol* (rape) and *violence* (violence), any form of sexual aggression – and we have seen

Table 1   Proportion of women reporting domestic violence during the last 12 months, according to partnership situation at the time of the survey (%)

Type of violence	With partner (n = 5,793)	No longer with partner (n = 115)	Total (n = 5,908)
Verbal insults and threats	4.0	14.8	4.3
among which repeated	*1.6*	*8.1*	*1.8*
Emotional blackmail	1.7	8.2	1.8
Psychological pressure	36.5	59.4	37.0
among which repeated	*23.5*	*52.4*	*24.2*
among which psychological harassment[1]	*7.3*	*27.3*	*7.7*
Physical aggression	2.3	10.2	2.5
among which repeated	*1.3*	*6.9*	*1.4*
Rape and other forced sexual acts	0.8	1.8	0.9
Global indicator of domestic violence[2]	9.5	30.7	10.0

[1] To have experienced more than three forms of psychological pressure, one of which repeatedly.
[2] To have experienced psychological harassment or repeated insults, or emotional blackmail or physical or sexual abuse.
Field: Women aged 20 to 59 who were in a relationship with a partner during the 12 months preceding the survey.
Source: ENVEFF survey, 2000; *Population et sociétés*, no. 364 (Jan. 2001), p. 3.

how that notion is constantly expanded – is assimilated to a violation of the self, to a kind of rape. Without going as far as Dworkin and MacKinnon, who liken pornography to rape and even compare it to slavery, to lynching, to torture and to the Holocaust, more and more voices can be heard equating sexual harassment and rape. For example, the psychiatrist Samuel Lapastier, the author of several studies on sexual harassment, declares in *l'Express*: 'Sexual harassment has to be considered as the equivalent of rape, moral constraint replacing physical coercion. It is an incestuous kind of rape; the hierarchical superior, in a position of authority is the incarnation of the parental image.'[21] But is this also the case with the new definition of sexual harassment that extends to colleagues and to subordinates? According to the psychia-trist, in sexual harassment there is 'more the need to humili-ate the woman and to debase her than that of seeking pleasure'. But confronted with the question 'How should you react to a harasser?' he answers in the following way: 'the more you resist, the better it is. You have to talk back to him, to remind him of the terms of the law: "this kind of thing is prohibited. I don't want this." The harasser is like a vicious little boy: you can resist him.' And this is indeed the essential difference between harassment and rape. What woman can resist a strong man who has decided to rape her in an isolated place?

The lawyer Emmanuel Pierrat has developed the same analogy from the point of view of the plaintiffs: 'On the topic of sexual harassment, the analogy with a certain discourse on rape [. . .] is still in order. The arguments of the defence are the same: the victim has provoked him, she has enjoyed it [. . .]. It is striking to find the same ingredients are present in most cases of sexual offences or crimes, whether rape, harass-ment or paedophilia: the denigration of the victims, the abuser's feeling of impunity, leading to frequent repetitions of the acts.'[22]

Finally, others assimilate prostitution to rape. Amalga-mating the many different forms of prostitution, prohibition-ists do not distinguish between sex slaves under the control of Mafiosi pimps and independent operators. This is the case, for example, of the Collectif Féministe contre le Viol [Feminist collective against rape], which affirms: 'In rape and in prostitution there is the same appropriation of women's bodies by men. The system of prostitution is in itself a sexist and sexual form of violence that should be judged side by side with other forms of violence against women, such as rape and domestic violence.'[23] To emphasize its point, the Collective details the calls received at the helpline Viols Femmes Informations [Rape information exchange for women] and concludes that 'the main point of entry into prostitution is rape, since 80 per cent of prostitutes have been subject to sexual violence in childhood.'[24] This figure of 80 per cent that

prohibitionists constantly mention in writing is rarely qualified by necessary explanations, that is, that this percentage
only applies to those who resort to the various relevant agen-
cies and the social services. This is far from being the case for
all prostitutes. In truth, the numbers put forward mask an
ideological bias that takes it for granted that providing sexual
services is the summit of female humiliation and is therefore
identical to rape. While it is legitimate for women who have
been raped to complain of the offence that has been committed against them, many prostitutes reject this amalgamation.
In order to shut them up, the status of 'absolute victims' has
been invented for them, silencing them. Whereas any statement from women is worth gold, the prostitute's word is
worth peanuts. She is considered from the outset as either a
liar or as subject to manipulation. It is a cavalier way to dis-
regard her objections, a contemptuous way of considering
her. Even if they vehemently deny this, prohibitionists are
waging a war against prostitutes. For as soon as the latter
reject the image of victim that the well-meaning wish to
saddle them with, they endanger many of the theories on sexuality that are being advanced today.

Statistics at the service of ideology

The widening of the concept of sexual aggression inevitably
leads to the growth of sex crimes and offences. The difficulties faced by women who press charges when they have been
raped or been subjected to assault and battery by a partner
are well known. Paradoxically, we must therefore rejoice
that rape accusations increase yearly, since this demonstrates
that we no longer allow this ignominy to go unpunished.
Moreover, it is well known that such figures do not reflect the
real number of actual rapes. A woman who has been raped
(whether by someone known to her, or not) needs great
courage in order to set in motion the whole police and judi-
cial process: the repetition (*ad nauseam*) of the gestures of
the humiliation and the suffering experienced, the years of
waiting, the public trial.

From this point of view, we must give homage to the contemporary feminism that has given rape its true signification and has done so much to wrest its victims from their solitude and from their silence. It is often thanks to the associations that listen to them and give them support that many of them find the courage to press charges.

This crime, largely underestimated in every country, has however sometimes been subject to astonishing estimates by the most radical feminists. Catharine MacKinnon affirms that 'the facts have to do with the rate of rape and attempted rape of American women, which is 44 per cent [. . .] some 4.5 per cent of all women are victims of incest by the father, an additional 12 per cent by other male family members, rising to a total of 43 per cent of all girls before they reach the age of eighteen.'[25] These calculations are not easy to understand and what has given rise to these figures is not known, so that one has the right to suspect some form of manipulation. The obvious objective is to demonstrate that one American woman out of two is the victim of the worst kind of male violence and that this is not the exception but the rule, the norm. This authorizes talk of a *rape culture*, even to see in rape a 'normal form of male behaviour'.

In 1985, the great magazine *Ms* published a study that caused a stir in the academic world. It was a commission given to a professor of psychology, Mary Koss, known for her orthodox feminism.[26] According to this study, conducted on campuses, one in four female students had been a victim of rape or attempted rape. But, among these victims, only a quarter actually called what had happened to them 'rape'. Additionally, Koss had asked the 3,000 young girls who were questioned: 'Have you given in to sex play (fondling, kissing, petting but not intercourse) when you didn't want to, because you were *overwhelmed* by a man's continual arguments and pressure?'[27] The 53.7 per cent who answered yes were counted as an implicit reserve of sexual victims.

'One in four' became the official statistic cited in women's studies departments, in feminist journals, anti-rape associations and by politicians. Susan Faludi and Naomi Wolf, two

stars of American feminism, used it as a slogan. A professor at
the School of Social Welfare at the University of California at
Berkeley, Neil Gilbert, and a young postdoc from Princeton,
Katie Roiphe, were the first to question the validity of these
statistics. The former showed that Koss's questions were far
too ambiguous and the interpretation of the answers was
biased.[28] He was surprised that 73 per cent of the young
women classified as raped refused to consider themselves as
such, and that 42 per cent of them continued to have sexual
relations with their so-called rapist. Finally, he pointed out
that despite the many campaigns against rape on campus and
the opening of support centres, in 1990 only two rape accusations were lodged with the police, while 14,000 female students attended UC Berkeley at that time. Roiphe made the
same observations about Princeton. When this was the only
thing the students spoke about, how could you explain that
there were so few complaints? She asked 'if 25 per cent of my
women friends are really being raped, wouldn't I know it?'[29]
She went on to publish a book on the new victim feminism
and its vision of sexual relations. *The Morning After: Sex, Fear
and Feminism on Campus* earned her great public recognition
and the hatred of the militants. She was denounced as a
traitor and a lackey of patriarchy. As for Neil Gilbert, he
became the object of boycotts and denunciations. On the
Berkeley campus, students protested, chanting: 'cut it out or
cut it off.' Some brandished signs that read KILL NEIL
GILBERT.[30]

As the situation became troubled, new studies on rape
started to be published. The National Women's Study (1992)
concluded that one American woman in eight (in other
words, 12 per cent) had been raped. Louis Harris put the
number at 3.5 per cent. Other studies had even lower figures
and did not attract big headlines in the press. It is clear: what
is at stake in the statistics is more political than scientific. The
greater the percentage of rape, the more widely the idea of a
sexist and misogynist American culture and of a particularly
violent American male could be spread.

In France, the Enveff study on violence against women

published more convincing figures. The global
sexual aggression measuring the proportion of ·
admitted having been subjected at least once to un.,.
sexual contact, attempted rape or rape in the course of the
year, in all possible contexts (in a public space, the workplace
or the home), in the year 2000 came to 1.2 per cent of the
total of women who were asked. Rape affected 0.3 per cent
of those women. Applying this percentage to the 15.9 million
women between twenty and fifty-nine living in metropolitan
France (using the 1999 census), the survey team concludes:
'this means that some 48,000 women of that age would have
been victims of rape within the year.'[31] This result does not
take into account the rape of minors and suggests that only 5
per cent of the rapes of adult women are ever reported.

These statistics are so serious that they should be used with
caution. So it is rather surprising to see the way the Collectif
Féministe contre le Viol wields them in their 2002 bulletin.[32]
In a boxed text announcing the results of the Enveff study, it
says:

- 11.4 per cent of women have been victim of at least one sexual
  aggression in the course of their life (touching up, attempted rape
  and rape):
      34 per cent before the age of 15;
      16 per cent between the ages of 15 and 17;
      50 per cent adults over 18.
- 8 per cent of women have been subject to at least one rape or
  attempted rape (a third of them minors).

Where do these figures come from? They are not in the
Enveff study dedicated to twenty to fifty-nine year olds. What
are the sources for the reports of violence against minors?
Was it the result of an extrapolation made from calls made to
their helpline? But, if that was the case, why not mention it
specifically instead of mixing up these percentages with those
of the national survey of 7,000 women? As for the 8 per cent
of women raped or having been subject to an attempted rape,
it is unclear how this figure is reached on the basis of the
survey results alone.

Even if we accept this figure of 8 per cent, this is not the end of the bad news. Two articles reviewing a television documentary on rape (based on the real story of Marie-Ange Le Boulaire, a journalist and the director of the documentary) mention different figures.[33] 'One woman in eight in France has been subjected to rape', we read, but this no longer adds up to 8 per cent but to 12 per cent. It is a statistic that we find on page 4 of the book the director has dedicated to the topic. In the book in question, Marie-Ange Le Boulaire writes: 'one woman in eight has been subjected or will be subjected to a sex attack during the course of her life.'[34] However, not every form of sexual aggression is actually rape, as the distinct categories of the Enveff survey make clear. We cannot put an undesired pawing on the same level as a rape in a parking lot by a twenty-three year old man armed with a knife. Contrary to what we are led to believe, the trauma involved in each of these cases is not the same. Why then inflate the statistics for rape, by their very nature so difficult to uncover, if not to exploit excessively the image of woman as victim and man as violent?

The statistics for sexual harassment call for the same type of remarks. When announcing the forthcoming European legislation on sexual harassment we have already discussed, the Commissioner Anna Diamantopoulou reminded us that '40 to 50 per cent of European women have received undesired sexual attention' and that 'in certain states the figures are 80 per cent'.[35] Leaving aside the 'stolen kiss' dear to Trénet and Truffaut, what should be included in the category of 'undesired sexual attention'? A misplaced gesture? A word too far? A look that is too insistent? But, as Katie Roiphe puts it very well, the difficulty with these new rules is that undesired sexual attention is part of nature and even of culture: 'To find wanted sexual attention you have to give and receive a certain amount of unwanted sexual attention. Clearly the truth is that if no one was ever allowed to risk offering unsolicited sexual attention, we would all be solitary creatures.'[36]

The consequence of these developments is the generalization of female victimhood and male culpability. Without going as far as A. Dworkin or C. MacKinnon, what is implied is that woman takes on more and more the status of a child: weak and powerless. More precisely, an innocent child, as the child used to be conceived before Freud redefined children as 'polymorphously perverse' creatures. The child oppressed by adults against whom it can do nothing. It is a return to the stereotypes of a previous era – to the time of the old patriarchy – when women, for ever minors, called for the men of the family to protect them. Except that today there are no more men to protect them. 'Viriarchy' has replaced 'patriarchy'. All men are suspect and their violence is exercised everywhere. The child-woman has to give herself up to the protection of the justice system, just as a child looks to its parents for protection.

The worst thing about this approach is obviously not the denunciation of violence against women, but the cause that has been assigned to this violence. It is no longer a question of denouncing the obsessed, the bad and the perverse. The evil is much deeper because it is general and concerns half the human race. It is the very principle of virility that stands accused. MacKinnon and Dworkin can well affirm that male dominance is the effect of our culture, the collective accusation 'always and everywhere' giving it the semblance of being natural, innate and universal, and this is what horrifies. We must change man, we are told, in other words change his sexuality, because that is what grounds the oppression of women within the social system.

In France, we take care not to accuse male sexuality too openly.[37] But little by little, a consensus was reached among academics to consider relations between men and women as social relationships and to make 'male domination'[38] into the *ultima ratio* for women's misery. On 8 March 2002, on the occasion of International Women's Day, Francine Bavay and Geneviève Fraisse published in *Le Monde* an article entitled 'L'insécurité des femmes' [Women's insecurity] that served as an opportune reminder of all these issues. 'Violence is gendered', they wrote, 'because theft as well as rape is committed mainly by men [. . .]. Violence is gendered, expression of a society that is, everywhere in the world, structured by male domination.' And they go on to mention the 'brute facts, from rape to stoning, from sexual harassment to prostitution, from insults to contempt, which are the repeated signs of a power of domination'.

Even if the unconditional denunciation of the male sex is denied in principle, it has in fact replaced the condemnation of male abuse. One side is Woman, powerless and oppressed; on the other Man, violent, domineering and exploiting. There they are, the one and the other, fixed in their opposition. How can we ever manage to free ourselves from this trap?

Philosophical malaise

Post-Beauvoirian feminism is something heterogeneous, even contradictory. The only point on which its practitioners agree is criticizing its originator. Beauvoir is said to have misunderstood sexual difference, denied the existence of female identity and preached an abstract universalism that, in reality, only masks a male universal.[39] And so she is said to have contributed despite herself to the production of an illusion that served to alienate women even more, since it encouraged them to align themselves with their masters. Simone de Beauvoir and her disciples appear to be guilty of virilism, moved by the 'desire to efface women's difference', and to have fallen into 'the trap of androcentrism.'[40] A little bit more and they would stand accused of treason and misogyny.

It is true that *The Second Sex* sidestepped femininity. It is equally true that Simone de Beauvoir stubbornly refused to define woman through motherhood. But critics have been a little quick to forget that by putting biology in its rightful place – second – she flung open the doors of women's prison. In other words, all those sexual stereotypes derived from an all-powerful nature. By championing the cause of freedom against natural necessity, she contributed to a change in mentalities and played a role in having women's right to contraception and abortion recognized. If all women celebrate this, some pretend not to know that this revolutionary right has sanctioned once and for all the primacy of culture over nature.

For it is surely here that the theoretical problem of the new feminism lies. How to redefine female nature without falling once again into the old clichés? How is it possible to talk about 'nature' without endangering freedom? How can the dualism of the sexes be sustained without rebuilding the prison-house of gender? The answers to these difficult questions are multiple and in opposition to each other. Even if the majority rejects loud and clear any return to essentialism, the dualism demanded by contemporary discourse leads to unsatisfying intellectual acrobatics. Whether opting for a little bit of culture and a lot of nature, or the reverse, every female or male critic suggests a model for the relationship between the sexes that fails to take into account all its possible consequences. Heterogeneous demands that must be theoretically justified after the fact are in fashion. Too bad if the philosophical explanation does not suit all of them. That was the case when parity was imposed in French politics. When the inscription of gender dualism had to be legitimated in the Constitution, many partisans of parity turned a blind eye. Such progress was well worth forgetting one's principles for.

Naturalism and oppositional dualism

'Equality in difference' is the general word of the day. It is possible, we are told, because that is what we want. Françoise Héritier can well point out that sexual difference has always and everywhere manifested itself as a hierarchy that is to the advantage of men, and that this grid is immutable and archaic since it survives even in the most evolved societies.[41] She nevertheless concludes that this universal phenomenon is cultural and therefore can be modified. Having dedicated a first volume to this 'differential valuing of the sexes', which she explained by men's will to control female procreation,[42] she realized a few years later that at last she held the solution that would put an end to this eternal male domination:

If women have been put under tutelage and dispossessed of the status of legally autonomous persons that men possess, in order to be confined to the imposed status of breeders, it is by gaining their freedom in the domain [of procreation] that they will simultaneously acquire dignity and autonomy. The right to contraception, with all it carries with it – consent, the right to choose her spouse, the right to divorce regulated through legal means and not simply through repudiation, outlawing the marriage of prepubescent daughters, etc. – the right of disposing of her own body constitutes the essential point of leverage because it acts at the very heart of the space where domination has been produced.[43]

The right to contraception as a solution to the liberation of women: how can we fail to be surprised by such a tardy revelation? In 1996 Françoise Héritier invokes in passing, in her conclusion, the progress that the mastery over reproduction represents, but this is immediately qualified by a mention of the lack of progress in 'minds and in the systems of representation'.[44] Do we need a reminder that the right to contraception dates back to 1967, the right to abortion to 1975 and that other Western democracies recognized these rights considerably before we did? But, if Western women have been controlling reproduction for more than thirty-five years, how can we continue to affirm that male domination remains universal? Is there not a confusion here between the historical phenomenon of male supremacy, effectively beaten back by contraception, and our supposedly archaic way of thinking? Françoise Héritier is right to insist on our universal tendency to think difference in terms of hierarchy and inequality, but she is perhaps wrong to link this to male appropriation of female fertility.[45] This is no longer in place and yet we still think difference in terms of inequality. This could mean that it is more difficult to get rid of that mental category than of male supremacy. Equality in difference is a wish, a utopia that would imply considerable progress for humanity in general, and not only for the male gender. As we can see, women are no less prisoners of this archaic category than men.[46] Even if it suits them to perceive it only in terms of a legitimate defence against the male *imperium*.

Since the end of the 1980s a great clamour has arisen from all sides in favour of the right to difference. This new right, claimed by all minorities, all communities, and by individuals themselves, has become the new battle cry for many feminists. According to them, the right to femininity itself would appear to be under attack. Virilized women are abandoning their identities, their freedoms and their values without realizing it. It was nothing less than an outcry against 'unisexual and matricidal democracies'[47] on their part. Some went as far as speaking of *gynocide*. The awful spectre of the indeterminacy of sex and gender reared its head once again. Even if there was not much risk of instituting a confusion between the sexes, an undifferentiated single gender, by definition male, and the destabilization of the duality of the sexes was feared. War on the One and its Multiple.

Antoinette Fouque has been constrained to bring women back to reason by announcing *Il y a deux sexes* [There are two sexes]. As for Sylviane Agacinski, she reminded them that 'the ideal of the reduction of difference, or as it's called, the "disappearance of gender", would constitute a totalitarian fantasy in aiming for a uniformization of individuals. There is nothing worse than the dream of a society of like individuals liberated from conflict by their very likeness.'[48]

All these lovely differences that distinguish us from men remain to be redefined, since male specificity appears to be carved in stone. Men only seemed to be evolving, but in reality have not really changed. To every feminist gain, they respond with new modes of domination.[49] Cavemen and men today still have something in common. And so we return to good old Mother Nature and to the fundamentals. Antoinette Fouque reminds us of our maternal greatness (and our obligation?), something underestimated and occluded by the eternal enemy. It is high time for the proper recognition and valuing of this difference, which privileges women and makes them infinitely superior to their partners. It is this capacity to procreate that gives woman her humanity, her generosity and her moral superiority. Just as Luce Irigaray did a long time before her, Antoinette Fouque looks to the mother/daughter dyad for salvation:

> To renew the specific tie of the daughter to the mother is to attempt to blow up the fortress of the One, of monotheism, of the 'There is only one God', of monodemocracy [. . .] to make apparent the perversion of a universe that imposed patriarchy on us [. . .]. I think that this female genealogy of the transmission of practices, of apprenticeships, of capacities from mother to daughter [. . .] perhaps carries something else other than the old model [. . .]. Woman have a different kind of capacity, the capacity for an active openness which is linked to gestation.[50]

These words do not conceal the desire to reconstruct an oppositional dualism. On the contrary: 'The pregnancy of a woman, gestation, is the only natural phenomenon of acceptance by the body, and thus by the psyche, of a foreign body. It is the model for all grafting.'[51] So women (mothers) are endowed with a 'capacity for hospitality' and with virtues inscribed in their body, unknown to the majority of men.[52] You don't know whether to laugh or cry. Such an approach making biology into the basis for all virtues and gender roles, condemns in the same breath men and those women who do not know motherhood. Men are obviously a lost cause. But then you also read that Virginia Woolf might perhaps not have committed suicide had she been a mother, and that Lou Andreas-Salomé remained a mystic because she stopped 'on this side of procreation'. What of lesbians, sterile women or all those who decline motherhood? They are left to draw the obvious conclusions.

For Sylviane Agacinski as well, even more than the experience of sexuality, it is motherhood that anchors female identity. 'There is a sort of sex-consciousness [. . .] which accompanies the experience of procreation.'[53] But Agacinski does not draw ethical conclusions from this. She asks herself questions about the interdependence of the two sexes, notably in the generative act. In her eyes, mutual dependence between man and woman is natural. So she considers it self-evident that 'humanity is *naturally* heterosexual' and that human beings are '*generally* animated by desire for the other and depend on this other to procreate [. . .]. Exclusive interest in the same sex is accidental, a sort of exception – even a frequent one – that confirms the rule.'[54] She goes on to conclude: 'How to think about sexual difference when the sexes cease to depend upon each other, when they split apart, and when, instead of desire for the other sex, we encounter desire for the same, what today we call *homosexuality*.'[55] True to herself, she refuses 'to abandon the model of the mixed parental couple [heterosexual, because] filiation should remain based upon the male and female, masculine and feminine double origin'.[56]

Male/female dualism doubles up here with homo/hetero dualism. Even if doubt can legitimately be cast on the anchoring of the latter in nature – Freud has taught us that heterosexuality is no less problematic than homosexuality – the recourse to biology and to anatomy in order to resolve simultaneously the philosophical question of identity and the political question of the relation between the sexes signals the return of a naturalism in full force. If this doesn't unify the theorists of feminism, it presents the incomparable advantage of being simple and self-evident. The famous 'common sense' dear to public opinion reclaims its place after decades of being questioned and deconstructed.

The concept of male domination

For the last thirty years, male domination has been tirelessly tracked down. It is being spotted everywhere: in institutions, in private or professional everyday life, in sexual relations or in the unconscious. Androcentrism is everywhere: all the more fearsome since it goes forth in disguise. It can mutate, just like certain viruses. As soon as you think you are done with it, it replicates itself in a different way. Men will never willingly abandon the material and sexual privileges their domination of women affords them.

From pioneering works by Nicole-Claude Mathieu, Colette

Guillaumin and Christine Delphy,[57] to more recent studies on men,[58] sociologists and anthropologists studying gender are in agreement and all claim more or less forcefully that 'the male gender is the gender that is hegemonic and prevalent'.[59] According to Welzer-Lang, the existence of male domination has become evident today: there is a consensus 'in interpreting male/female relationships as sexual social relationships':

> the entire social sphere is divided according to the same symbolic structure which attributes to men and to masculinity noble functions and to women and to femininity tasks and functions of lesser value. This division of the world, this cosmogony based on gender is maintained and regulated by violence. These multiple and varied kinds of aggressive acts, ranging from men's domestic violence to rape committed in time of war right through violence in the workplace, tend to preserve the powers that men attribute themselves collectively and individually at the expense of women.[60]

And so it becomes as imperative to fight male domination as it is to fight racism and fascism.

Many questions arise: if male domination and the violence that founds it are as universal as they are said to be, where will salvation come from? From the men who identify as feminists? What can they suggest to their peers that will put an end to their position as exploiters? A collective awakening followed by a bout of self criticism? But could this really produce a reversal in mentalities, forms of behaviour and institutional arrangements? The difficulty comes from the formulation of the evil. Of course, care is taken not to invoke a masculine *nature* that would prevent any hope of change and offer no solution other than an unthinkable separatism, but the universality of this kind of talk fixes and 'essentializes' this traditional masculinity. The leader of the Bordeaux mosque, considered to be a liberal, concludes from this that 'male dominance is a fact, a "transcultural invariant"'.[61] He seeks to explain it by an 'irreducible difference, the famous Y chromosome'. Leaving aside the Y chromosome, where does this masculinity seeped in the will to dominate come from?

Some say that its origin is to be found in man's eternal jealousy of the reproductive power of woman; for others, it is linked to his sexuality. According to American radicals, a hard-on is a symbol of his power and the penis is a weapon which man uses all the better to possess and denigrate woman. Finally, for others, masculinity is a source of social advantage. Assimilating men to capitalists and women to the proletariat, it is noted that men only cede their power on minor points in order to preserve the essential. According to the sociologist François de Singly,

> it is possible to assert that male domination is promoted under the cover of 'neutralization'. The defeat of macho men is a misleading reality. One could say that the category of men has abandoned one territory the better to resist the offensive of the category of women. Men have lost what both men and women consider to be the primary male terrain, but they have succeeded in preserving all the other territories where they used to exercise their supremacy.

And Singly goes on to cite 'techniques of self-affirmation that are "neutral" such as science, computing and politics.'[62]

Reading these lines, discouragement takes hold. Male domination appears to be not only 'transcultural' but eternal. However, some refuse to give up. Without going as far as the solution suggested by the feminist thinker John Stoltenberg, who calls for the end of masculinity by 'refusing to be a man',[63] others put every hope in pedagogy and psychoanalysis. Terry Kupers, a psychiatrist and an activist in NOMAS (National Organization for Men Against Sexism), suggests 'redefining power in a way that would allow men to feel powerful without being sexist.'[64] For his part, Daniel Welzer-Lang prefers the solution championed by Michael Kimmel, spokesman for NOMAS: 'Men should learn powerlessness.'[65]

A double feeling of unease remains. This relates as much to the means of diagnosis as to the proposed remedies. Despite what the more pessimistic might say, the condition of Western women has changed considerably, as has their behaviour. Would that make men the only section of humanity incapable of evolving? Is the male entity immutable? Unease, too, when facing a generalization that opposes two blocks: the category of women, the category of men. Does this not mean falling back into the trap of essentialism, against which feminists have fought so hard for their own benefit? There is not one universal masculinity, but many forms of masculinity, just as there are many forms of femininity. Binary categories are dangerous because they hide the complexity of reality in favour of simplistic and constraining schemas. Unease as well faced with the wholesale condemnation of one sex, something that looks very much like sexism. Unease, finally, as to the will to 're-educate men', something that brings back rather bad memories. The order of the day, whether implicit or explicit, is to 'change man' rather than 'fight against the abuses of some men'. This smacks of a totalitarian utopia. Sexual democracy, always imperfect, is obtained step by step.

Finally, it could be asked whether the simplifying and unifying notion of 'male domination' is not an obstructive concept. In the name of a radical alterity, it can be used to avoid working through complexity, historicity and the evolution of the relationship between the sexes. This 'catch-all' concept, locking men and women into two opposing camps, closes the door to any hope of understanding their mutual influence and of measuring their common humanity.

Manicheism

Oppositional dualism secretes a new hierarchy of the sexes that we are nevertheless claiming to rid ourselves of. A moral hierarchy is opposed to the object of the fight, the hierarchy of power. The dominating sex is identified with evil, the oppressed sex with good. This identification has been reinforced by the new status given to the victim, and in the first instance to the child victim.

In the 1990s, and notably after the Dutroux affair in 1997, paedophilia was finally recognized as a crime that had remained hidden for far too long. Everyone is being exhorted no longer to turn a blind eye and no longer to be an accomplice to such infamy. And so, reading the newspaper reports of that time, the dominant impression is of a sudden proliferation of paedophile crimes. Not one week passed by without yet another teacher, educationalist or priest being hauled in for questioning by the police. A sort of psychotic attitude was enacted towards all those whose work put them into contact with young children. It was at that point, on 26 August 1997, that Ségolène Royal, minister assigned to secondary education, published a circular. In it she reminded teachers of an obligation already specified in the Penal Code: 'As soon as a student confides to an employee of the state education department any incident that he or she claims has harmed him or her, it is a duty of that employee to *immediately* and *directly* advise the State Prosecutor.'[66] On the 8 o'clock television news, the minister explained this statement in person. The public understands that it is the duty of an employee of the state to act as an informer in such a cases because the child's word is sacred. On a television programme, Ségolène Royal proclaimed several times: 'The child tells the truth.'[67] Some child psychiatrists were splashed all over the media in order to make similar statements, and an association for the defence of abused children even demanded that 'a presumption of the credibility of a child's testimony' be inscribed in law.[68] Beyond a mere reactivation of the saying 'out of the mouth of babes', a more general principle of truth is brought to mind: *the victim is always right*. As Paul Bensoussan points out, 'the dominant current of thought insists on the belief that the victim obviously tells the truth by virtue of being a victim.'[69]

From child to woman there is but a short step. Both are innocent and powerless victims of aggressive and dominating man. A cause is surreptitiously added to the notion that the victim is always right. It is because the victim is the incarnation of good threatened by the power of evil. This Manichean vision engenders two kinds of consequences, both deriving from differentialism.

The first consequence, a radical one, is the call for separatism. Analysing very well the writings of feminist nationalism, 'a constant dimension of feminist movements', Liliane Kandel illuminates the double implication, ontological and moral, of such a current of thought.[70] The theme of *female nationalism*, as it was critiqued by Ti-Grace Atkinson in the beginning of the 1980s, supposes 'the unique quality of women's spirit, capacities and emotions that makes them into a radically distinct entity, which cannot be assimilated to men'. In a 1989 text, Luce Irigaray makes explicit the opposition between men and women and the idealization of the latter. 'Mankind [*le peuple des hommes*] wages war everywhere all the time with a perfectly clear conscience. Mankind is traditionally carnivorous, sometimes cannibalistic. So men must kill to eat, must increase their domination of nature.'[71] The nation of women, moulded by maternal virtue, is just the opposite. This feminism has a common cause with ecology and vegetarian philosophy. Take the following political recommendation: 'women will have the civil right to defend their lives and those of *their* children, *their* homes, *their* traditions against any unilateral decision based on men's laws [. . .]. Half of all media coverage will be specially aimed at women.' A little further on, she concludes: 'Half the citizens of the world are women. They must gain a civil identity with corresponding rights.'[72] In other words, a juridical system, founded on 'particular rights, specific to the group of women'. As L. Kandel says, a difference in rights is starting to take shape against the backdrop of the demand for the right to difference.

A second aspect of sexual Manicheism is expressed by another current of female nationalism that first appeared in the inaugural text of the MLF (Mouvement de Libération des Femmes – Women's Liberation Movement) in 1970. Affirming 'We are the people' (meaning the real people, the proletariat), 'women constituted as a subversive group par excellence, quasi messianic, [are] invested with the kind of mission which formerly fell to people in arms, or to the proletariat: Revolution, the eradication of all forms of oppression, and the dawning of a new humanity'.[73]

We would be wrong to see this as an old relic of the spirit of 1968. While the terminology is marked by the passage of time, the idea being transmitted is far from dead. If you think, as some do, that there is nothing to be expected from men, entrenched as they are in their culture of domination, salvation can only come from women, their victims, who possess a benevolent and peaceful nature.

More recently, it has been possible to see another example of this Manicheism appearing in France. On the occasion of the debate on parity in politics, which took place from 1992 to 1999, a certain number of themes that might have seemed already exhausted, returned in full force. From the start, parity was presented as a quasi-technical means to remedy the ridiculously small number of women elected to the National Assembly.[74] The solution that was proposed, equal access to seats, had the advantage of simplicity and a certain amount of statistical evidence. There was no question of differentialism or of female nature.

It was women politicians, from all sides of the political spectrum, who first took hold of the issue even before there was any talk of parity. As early as 1984–5, Mariette Sineau had conducted a survey among about forty of them and most of them insisted on their 'feeling for the human': 'A greater capacity for listening and empathy, a more committed presence at the grass-roots level [. . .] is already attributed to women who are active today on the political scene.'[75] After 1992, other famous women in politics justified parity with a reminder of their special qualities. According to Simone Weil, 'less careful of their personal ambitions, women want to act, to get concrete results. By taking more risks, by being less formal [. . .] they go forth with determination and courage in order to ensure that the cases they take on achieve a proper outcome.'[76] What is implied is that men think only of their personal ambition, couldn't care less about the results and lack courage. Martine Aubry sings the same tune when she finds that women have their feet on the ground 'because they are more interested in action than in power'. They can therefore bring about 'another way of doing politics, more concrete, closer to the people.'[77] This is also the opinion of Elisabeth Guigou, who enumerates at length the virtues of activists, 'courageous, tenacious, devoted', and those of the women who exercise power, who put their ideas before their ambition; 'all a little bit rebellious', they can distance themselves from power, pomp and decorum.[78] In sum they are much more friendly than their male colleagues. But Elisabeth Guigou takes an extra step by making use of the arguments of differentialist feminism, and in particular those of Antoinette Fouque. Convinced by her theory about the irreducible difference between the sexes, linked to procreation, she concludes: 'one must recognize that there are two sexes [. . .] carriers of fecundity and of hope. It is a first step towards symbolic differentiation: two sexes, two ways of seeing the world',[79] and thus of doing politics.

It is true that the Manicheism that comes out of the arguments of some of the supporters of parity has never taken on the more provocative aspects of separatist feminism. But by constantly repeating that women are less warmongering, less vain, more down to earth, more preoccupied by others, more devoted to the struggle for life and for freedom, a caricature in reverse of men is being drawn. Surreptitiously, the maternal ideal appears once again to justify both the moral superiority of women over men, and their prerogatives. And all this without any opposition from other supporters of parity who are usually against these kinds of arguments.

All these discourses have been in circulation for several years and have given birth to what one could call a female political correctness. Woman is simultaneously an incarnation of the victim of male society and of a courageous little soldier who repairs the damage caused by men. In an article titled 'Courage, les ravaudeuses! [Courage, menders]', Christine Clerc gives a perfect illustration: 'Men are in a crushing majority in government as well as in Parliament, and everywhere they draw up amendments that bear their name and betray laws, a great number of laws [. . .]. As for women, they not only staff thousands of associations that take care of the aged, the ill, the socially excluded, the victims of violence, adolescents and refugees' – the elected women have a social conscience: 'They watch over everything and everyone [. . .].

And they do this at great risk to themselves.' And she goes on to pay tribute pell-mell to the courage of J. Fraysse, Mayor of Nanterre, and to the everyday courage of the women elected in Agen, Strasbourg, Beauvais and Amiens. Not to mention Paris, where a woman, Anne Hidalgo, came first in line as soon as the mayor, Bertrand Delanoe, the victim of a stabbing, had to stand down. Hats off, conquerors! Well done, menders.[80]

Courage, a sense of sacrifice, devotion, such are the virtues of the good mother who by definition knows nothing of the vices and the drives of the bad father. But, looking at it more closely, it is possible to point to a more nuanced and complex reality than oppositional dualism allows. In the year 2000, official statistics announced that 83,800 children were at risk.[81] On 8 December 2002, the minister in charge of the elderly stated that 800,000 old people were being mistreated. Are men really the only ones in whose care children and the elderly are left?

The amalgam is not a good tool for acquiring knowledge. And the collective condemnation of one sex is an injustice deriving from sexism. To make violence the unfortunate preserve of men, to confuse the normal and the pathological, leads one to a biased diagnosis, and this does not bode well for a good prescription.

2
Omissions

Every form of militancy comes up against a difficulty: the problem of taking into account the varied nature of reality.

Recent French and European reports on domestic violence against women display alarming statistics linked with striking comparisons. According to a Council of Europe publication, one woman in five in Europe is a victim of violence, and in most cases she is attacked by a member of her family.[1] Domestic violence appears to be the principal cause of death or disability 'ahead of cancer, of road accidents, even of war'. In France, six women die every month as a result of domestic violence. In Spain, a woman is killed almost every week by her husband or her partner: 'domestic terrorism has caused three times more victims there in the last year than attacks by ETA [the Basque separatist movement].' The number of French women who were victims of domestic violence in 2001 is cited, 1,350,000, in other words 10 per cent of women,[2] as well as the number of Spanish women, 2 million, or 11 per cent of the country's female population. There is talk of murder, of battered women and of violent husbands, but without going into any more detail. But we have seen, at least in the French study, that the concept of violence includes not only physical aggression, but also the psychological pressures that account for the greatest number of violent domestic acts. According to psychologists, repeated psychological and verbal aggression can be considered as destructive as physical violence.

Reading these statistics might make us think that there is a new epidemic of male violence underway. There seems to be hardly any difference between Europe and more disadvantaged continents. At this point, the hasty reader or the one already convinced of men's natural malevolence becomes despondent. But several questions can be raised. Since every European country recognizes divorce, how come so many women, subjected only to psychological pressures,[3] do not take advantage of it? How come they don't simply pack their bags? The most obvious answer has to do with the lack of material resources: women who are mothers may find it financially impossible to see to their own and to their children's needs. However, the Council of Europe's report tells us that 'poverty and lack of schooling are not significant factors; the incidence of domestic violence even seems to rise with the level of financial resources and education.' A Dutch study, cited by the author of the European text, reveals that almost all the perpetrators of the violent acts aimed at women hold a university degree. This does not mean that the victims do so as well, but nevertheless the passivity of the women (or men) who might escape their tormentor but do not do so comes as a surprise.[4] Paradoxically, it is battered men who will, a little further along, provide us with an answer.

On the other hand, when you read that 50,000 French women are raped every year, that 41,000 Spanish women made an official complaint against violent husbands in 2001, and that in Greece one in four men between the ages of twenty-five and thirty-five has beaten his partner at least once, you ask yourself what these violent men should be called? Psychopaths? Sadists? Bastards? Or should you think, on the contrary, that violence is inherent in a masculinity always defined by the desire for domination? In other words, is male violence a pathology or is it the skidding of a drive that is characteristic of men?

The unthinkable

Legal statistics show that the percentages of male and female violence are quite stable. Of those convicted of voluntary manslaughter or assault and battery, 86 per cent are men.[5] The lack of symmetry between men and women is such that, apart from psychologists and psychoanalysts, few show any interest in female violence. For feminists, the subject is taboo. Anything that diminishes the impact of the concept of male domination and of female victimhood is unthinkable and unthought. When it is spoken of, it is always in the same way: first, that female violence is insignificant; then, that it is always a response to male violence; finally, that this violence is legitimate. Thus, according to Sylviane Agacinski,

> violent women are always rebels, resisters, revolutionaries, sometimes also terrorists: in general their violence is a counterviolence. Outside these contexts, criminologists have remarked that a man who kills a women – often *his* woman – takes the violent appropriation of the other to its conclusion, even when he loves her. While, the woman who kills, in most cases, completes a process of liberation.[6]

The same explanation is to be found in Françoise Héritier's writings[7] or in those of the militant sociologist Daniel Welzer-Lang, who admits to his 'anger faced with the arguments of those who render symmetrical the oppression of women and men's lived experience, the violence to which women are subject and the few women who are violent, often out of vengeance or despair, towards their partners'.[8] Even more revealing is the collective work called *De la violence des femmes* [Of female violence] edited by Cécile Dauphin and Arlette Farge.[9] The introduction does indicate that it is a subject painful to feminists and that to 'deal with this reality might appear to some unjustifiable, because it compromises "the cause of women" as well as the necessary condemnation of violence against women'. However, not one of the ten articles written by serious historians or academic feminists deals with the subject in and of itself.[10] Some do not even mention it at all.

It is all about reminding the reader of male violence, from which women's violence flows. Thus the article Dominique Godineau dedicates to the 'citizens, rabble-rousers and furies of the guillotine'[11] clearly signals both the pro-revolutionary tradition's embarrassed silence on the subject, and the very strong impression that a reading of the archives gives us of female violence. However, the author herself labours to diminish its impact. First, she notes that the archives – those of the repression – were written by the police, in other words, by men. So it can be supposed that their perception of events included 'a component of exaggeration or misrepresentation'. Then she argues that the violence of the women was above all a verbal violence. They excited the men so as to incite them to revolution. Are not 'the cries of fury', 'the horrible vociferations' that they were accused of in 1795, also 'a form of verbal violence done to women'? As to their behaviour in front of the guillotine, 'it is only the expression of their barbarous joy and excessive emotion' faced with the symbol of the supreme power of the people against their enemies. 'So, for women excluded from the practice of legal violence (national guard, revolutionary tribunal, etc.), to be present during an execution was one of the only means at their disposal that could assure them of the possession of the power of the people, and even of their symbolic participation in it.'

Dominique Godineau has produced a political reading of women's violence under the Revolution. She wanted to counter the image of a ferocity particular to women. However, at the end of her article, she seems overcome by regret:

> I would not wish, for that matter, to blunt any edges and to present an image that is too sugary, too policed. Women revolutionaries have indeed been violent. They have shouted. They have promised death to their enemies, sometimes they have given it, they have gone to see it. They have terrified. Like the others.

It is this *like the others* that is the most interesting, and about which we are not to know more.

Truth be told, female violence is difficult to think, not only for reasons having to do with militancy – perhaps violence has no sex – but because it endangers the self-image of women. When the philosopher Monique Canto-Sperber writes of her surprise at a Palestinian woman becoming a suicide bomber, she imagines four possible reasons for her confusion:

> Is it because the horror of a death where you blow yourself up is even more unbearable when the body of a woman is its victim? Is it because this supposes an undifferentiated violence towards others and oneself that I could ill imagine in a woman? Is it because I imagine that a woman should be more compassionate for the concrete suffering of her victims than a man? Or is it because I believe that women are more realist, less subject to fanaticism, to the intoxication of the cause?[12]

Three of the hypotheses cited are based on the conviction of an essential difference between men and women. Through nature or culture, the latter should be strangers to the violence of the former. It is this postulate that dominates most current work on violence. In the name of a statistical asymmetry, there is a refusal to raise the question of female violence and abuse of power. However, it is precisely this subject that we must now broach.

Women's violence

In history or in everyday life, female violence is difficult to unearth. Not that it doesn't exist: there is regular mention in the press of violent acts committed by women. It is simply that it has long been ignored or downplayed. That is the case for example with the participation of women in two of the worst genocides[13] of the twentieth century: those that took place in Nazi Germany and in Rwanda. It is also the case with the female protagonists of various news items about violence, which give rise to astonishment rather than reflection.

Historical violence

It was by way of a remarkable collective work in homage to Rita Thalmann[14] that we discovered the question of the participation of women in the deployment of genocide. In an introductory article titled 'Femmes, féminismes, nazisme, ou: On ne naît pas innocent(e), on le devient [Women, feminisms, Nazism: or, one is not born innocent, one becomes it]', Liliane Kandel observes that for almost forty years German feminists and historians have shown little interest in the topic. She comments on 'the undeniable difficulty that historians, researchers or militant feminists have in approaching these questions[...]. Or, more precisely, in approaching them *from this angle.*'[15] However, twenty of them, French and German women, have had the courage to pose disturbing questions on 'the degree of connection and the modes of participation, whether active or passive, open or hidden, limited or sustained'[16] of the accomplices of the regime, instead of concentrating only on the activities of the members of the resistance or on the female victims of Nazism. In sum, they entered into feminism's 'grey areas'.

We find that the dominant idea that 'women were not involved in the Nazi enterprise and remained uncompromised by it' is thereby put in question. The volume examines the way in which Aryan feminists were able to renounce their 'sisterhood' with their Jewish friends and fellow activists, as well as the modes of the effective and conscious participation of women in the various aspects of the system of expropriation, plunder and denunciation of German Jews. It also looks at the case of women directly or explicitly engaged in the ideological and material system of persecution: women in the SS, intellectuals and academics, such as the biologist Agnes Bluhm who unhesitatingly supported Hitler's regime. In other words, it deals with 'Hitler's zealous executioners',[17] whose number also included a great many women. In sum, this book puts an end to the myth of female innocence summed up in the following way by Claudia Koonz: 'Men were Nazis, and the women were innocent.'

Nicole Gabriel, who has worked on the regime's informants, following Helga Schubert's book *Judasfrauen*,[18] puts forward the following interesting typology. She distinguishes those who have become informants 'through civic duty', through loyalty towards the regime; those who have acted 'to create order', to resolve private conflicts to their advantage; and finally those who did so out of passion, motivated by their drives, because they were looking for a libidinal enjoyment in the act of harming another.[19] This last category should hold our attention because it sheds light on a motivation we wish to see as foreign to women, in other words, on sadism. By suspending a certain number of prohibitions, particularly those concerning physical violence, National Socialism served as an 'outlet for an existing potential for aggression. Aggression could express itself through an experience of enjoyment in face of the spectacle of violence or else in an actual participation in violence',[20] in the street, for example, by breaking windows or by hitting people. By reminding us that for both genders denunciation is the weapon of the weak, one that allows 'killing with words', in all impunity, Nicole Gabriel rightly talks in terms of a letting loose of sadistic drives.

In a study of SS women, Gudrun Schwarz asks herself what part they played in the process of persecution and extermination, according to whether they were wives, daughters or sisters of members of the SS, members of the female corps of the SS or guards in a camp.[21] It is in the archives of Koblenz that she found evidence of the latter category. In 1945, women guards numbered 3,817, in other words they made up 10 per cent of the personnel. These guards carried out their duty in women's concentration camps as well as in extermination camps such as Auschwitz-Birkenau and Lublin-Maidanek. Every camp was led by a male member of the SS, but the guards exerted a direct authority over the detainees. Responsible for the day-to-day harassment and tormenting of female prisoners, they had the right to carry arms during their service and were an embodiment of power. As they themselves admitted during their trial, they were participants in the selection processes. In Auschwitz or Maidanek, all these women, feared for their brutality and their zeal, 'directly served a system of oppression and of death [. . .] and laboured to ensure the flawless functioning of the system of extermination. A survivor of the Gross-Rosen concentration camp who was called to testify as a witness declared: 'it was the German civilians who beat us. The [female] SS guards had nothing against this. They beat and tortured us as much as they could.'

Gudrun Schwarz drily concludes that despite the number of existing files, women have not been the object of independent research 'in the field of women's studies, nor in that of research on the SS'.[22]

It is still much more difficult to know the real part that Rwandan women played in the genocide of 1994. Of the 120,000 people accused of genocide, 3,564 are women. It is true that they only constitute 3.5 per cent of the total of those who committed genocide, and it is too soon for the historians to do their work. But how can we not be struck by the media silence surrounding them? A notable exception, however, is a five-page article by a special correspondent of *Elle* magazine, Caroline Laurent.[23] She has met these silent Hutu women, accused of having 'pillaged, denounced, tortured, handed over, incited to rape, killed' members of the Tutsi community. They have been identified as guilty by the survivors and by 'witnesses who have recounted the violence of the machete blows, of the rapes, the collective massacres in the churches, the hunting down of men, women and children' in which women have participated. According to the president of the Association of the Widows of the April Genocide (Avega) whose husband was denounced by a neighbour and never returned, women's involvement was 'massive and decisive'. And it was totally premeditated by the ideologists of the genocide. Women's participation was indispensable to the success of their evil project. Thus, intellectuals, doctors, professors, nuns, mothers and farmers joined the ranks of those who committed genocide. 'Without women's participation, there would not have been as many victims.'

These words are corroborated in the report *African Rights* put together on the basis of the testimony of those who escaped, and entitled 'Less innocent than they appear: when women become murderers'.

After sharing many testimonies, each one more terrible than the next, the journalist puts the question of female barbarity to Professor Serban Ionescu,[24] presently researching the Rwandan genocide. In his answer, he describes the climate of extreme tension and fear cultivated by those who planned the genocide, in order to condition the Hutus to combat the Tutsis. He tells of how women were mobilized, just like the men, by the mechanisms of identification with the aggressor, by group phenomena. Just like the men, 'they lost their humanity' in this way. He adds that if we find it so difficult to conceive of the idea of such female violence, it is because what is at work is 'a social stereotype, linked to the idealization of women and which fosters the idea that only men can commit such acts. By thinking like this, we are in denial, because we cannot bear to contemplate acts of that sort. In reality, the female potential for violence does exist; we see it in the participation of women in infanticide or in sexual abuse. In the Rwandan context, where the genocide was cleverly orchestrated, the massive participation of women in such acts is absolutely not something that is inconceivable.'[25]

Finally, we will note that the year 2003 saw the first condemnation of a European woman for crimes against humanity. On 27 February, the international war crimes tribunal at The Hague condemned the seventy-two year old former president of Bosnia, Biljana Plasvic, to eleven years of prison for her key role in the Serbian policy of ethnic cleansing during the Bosnian war of 1992 to 1995.

The violence of the everyday

Outside periods of exceptional violence, some women do kill, humiliate and torture.[26] They do not always kill out of disappointed love or to defend themselves against a violent husband. They do so as well out of self-interest or through sadism. They figure in a series of pathological exceptions to the general rule. However, an even more disturbing phenomenon seems to be growing in the last ten years and causes disbelief: the rise in the violent behaviour of adolescent girls.

This past year has been rich in news items involving very young girls. In March 2002, a fourteen-year-old adolescent was tortured by two companions of the same age, who kept at it until they left her for dead: slit wrists, hacked neck, knife wounds to the stomach, crushed face. In May, the county court of Haute-Garonne heard the case of Clémentine and Sandrine, aged twenty-two, accused of having kidnapped, robbed, whipped and attempted to strangle a nineteen-year-old student, leaving him for dead. All this was done under the leadership of a fearsome fourteen-year-old girl. In August, a young man of nineteen was taken prisoner for three weeks at Chateauroux and lived through a terrible ordeal (beaten, ears partly torn off, broken nose, burns on the body, multiple rapes), all inflicted by a group of drop-outs which included two girls. On 25 November 2002, an international day for the elimination of violence against women, *Libération* published two little stories. In Rouen, three young women between the ages of eighteen and twenty-four were condemned to four months in prison (suspended) and to two months (to serve) for having insulted, covered in spit and hit a bus driver. In Vitrolles, three women kicked and punched a twenty-year-old girl, burning her with cigarettes before parading her naked in the city for ten minutes, knocking on doors to show off their victim. In January 2003, in Hauts-de-Seine, a sixteen-year-old girl wounded her maths teacher in the thigh with a knife.

In September 1998, *Le Point* investigated girls' violence as a follow-up to a news item: adolescents between the ages of ten and sixteen attacked some fifty people before being arrested *in flagrante* – old ladies, adolescents of their own age, but also men at the height of their strength. Terms such as 'savagery' and 'ferocity' were bandied about. However, as Sophie Coignard notes, urban violence, girl style, is still a non-topic, even if all the experts in the field point to an emerging phenomenon. A July 1997 study by Renseignements Généraux noted that an increasing number of violent acts were committed by girls, whose motives for getting into fights were quite similar to those of boys: debts of honour, stolen clothes, love rivalries, scams detrimental to other girls. The Marseilles police department estimated these acts to amount to 1.78 per cent in 1997 and 2.43 per cent in 1998.[27]

It is a derisory figure compared to the delinquency of adolescent boys, even if, as some experts maintain, it is underestimated. The director of the Institut des Hautes Études de la Sécurité Intérieure, Philippe Melchior, observes that 'we would be less inclined to give a criminal interpretation to the same offence if a girl committed it rather than a boy'. He notes that very violent young girls leave the professionals 'despairing and unbelieving'.[28] This is because of our age-old prejudices, explains Sophie Body-Gendrot, professor and expert in urban politics at Sciences-Po and at the Sorbonne, 'just as it took us a long time to admit that children might be terribly violent, because the image of childhood is that of innocence'.[29]

The same thing was observed in the year 2000 in Canada, where the statistics of the last ten years signal a marked increase in the violent behaviour of young women. Even if adolescents are always responsible for the great majority of the violent offences committed by young people (and female adolescents are only responsible for a third of these), the number of female adolescents accused of violent crime has increased by 127 per cent compared to an increase of 65 per cent among male adolescents during the same period.[30] Similar trends are observed in the United States and in England. According to the Canadians, even if the forms of violence are different in boys and in girls, the risk factors are comparable: a history of family violence and aggression, difficulties in school, mental health troubles and low self-confidence. Indeed, as the report points out: 'nothing leads us to believe that girls or boys have different reasons for adopting aggressive and violent ways of behaving. *Young boys don't necessarily have a greater tendency to be violent or aggressive.* Culture and environment seem to be the best indicators of juvenile delinquency, rather than gender.'[31] We would observe that in certain neighbourhoods it is adolescent boys who impose a hierarchy based on force, imbued with a brutal machismo, one that leaves young girls no other solution than aggression. As Eric Debardieux, director of the Observatoire Européen de la Violence Scolaire, writes, 'female machismo is without a doubt one of the ways of resisting male domination.'[32] How can you defend yourself against the daily violence of the young gang leaders, against their verbal, physical and sexual aggression, other than by becoming feared yourself?

However, this well-documented case of a type of violence that is reactive to the violence of boys does not tell the whole story about female delinquency. Girls mainly attack other girls or women. Some experts, such as Philippe Melchior, suggest that it is a way of emancipating themselves:

> In a certain sense, it is normal that girls accede to a form of equality in aggression. The fact that girls' violence manifests itself above all in the confines of school, the only space of equality between the sexes as far as they are concerned, makes sense from that point of view. They scam, they threaten with knives, they attack the teachers just as the boys do. They accede to an identity that mirrors the characteristics of our society.[33]

Some might say that this is indeed proof that society is saturated with the model of male domination and girls submit to it. But if that were the case, the violence of adolescents would not be largely limited to areas where great social and cultural misery prevail. And, in the last resort, is it not rather poverty, with the serious psychological deprivations that often accompany it, that is the primary source of all the frustrations that engender violence? These are frustrations that are greater for boys than for girls in a society that only values economic and personal success, but they are frustrations that girls share more and more in a society that also proclaims the equality of the sexes. We can therefore bet that girls' violence will only increase under the double pressure of a frustration which is both social and sexist, not necessarily just one on its own.

Domestic violence

We have seen that domestic violence speaks in a male voice. So it comes as something of a surprise to discover in the Council of Europe's report cited above that there can also be male victims of domestic violence. According to official German statistics, 5–10 per cent of these kinds of violent acts are perpetrated by women who beat their husband. So much so that the first German refuge for battered men has opened in Berlin.

It is possible to find, here and there, some indication of this kind of thing in other countries,[34] but in France we pretend that it does not occur. The Enveff study is concerned exclusively with violence against women, and no one has had the idea of posing similar questions to men. Without questions, there can be no answers, and the total silence about the phenomenon makes it even more difficult to hear the complaint of 'battered men'. All the more so since the very expression engenders at best surprise and more often doubt, and even open mockery. After a long battle to have their mistreatment recognized, women can now take for granted that dedicated associations will listen to them, and that they will be taken more seriously by the police. Nothing of the sort is available to men. On the one hand, there is no symmetry between the violence they may have to endure and that which other men inflict on their companions. To date, there are no statistics showing that any man has died from the after-effects of domestic violence. On the other hand, the expression 'battered man' appears to be paradoxical. In the collective unconscious, and not only that of feminists, men either attack those who are weaker than they are, or else protect them. They are never imagined to be on the side of the victims, nor women on the side of tormentors or persecutors.

Disbelief about battered men is not only due to the small

number of them who declare themselves. It is similar to the scepticism already experienced by those women who might be able to get rid of their tyrant and do not do so.[35] Statistically, men are stronger than women and it is thought, rightly or wrongly, that they can always put a stop to their partner's violence. If they do not do so, it must be because of cowardice or masochism. It is not the kind of thing that would invite the sympathy of the public.

However, the motivations involved on either side are more complex than we might be led at first to believe. An interview with three battered men gives an indication of what they have in common with a great number of women in the same situation.[36] To be beaten is a humiliation that disintegrates a human being whatever their sex. Shame is felt in admitting to it, shame in confiding in someone about it, and so the tendency is to hide everything and let it go. Hervé, forty, lived through an ordeal for four years: he was kicked, punched, kneed. He went to work with a black eye or a split forehead. He would say that his little girl injured him with a toy. Christian, thirty-three, testified that violence was an everyday occurrence in his life. A wrong word or question, and he got a slap. Threatened several times with an iron or a hammer, he couldn't go to sleep for fear of being stabbed in bed. One day, pushed to the limit, he reacted violently and it was his companion who lodged a complaint for assault and battery against him! He says: 'Me, as a man, I couldn't see myself complaining.'

Just like battered women, these men seem to go on hoping for a long time that their situation will improve. Like many women, they appear mysteriously attached to their persecutor. But unlike them, they have at their disposal a physical strength that could protect them and that they rarely use.

The Enveff study estimates that 2.5 per cent of women suffer from the physical aggression of their partners. It is difficult to estimate the number of men who are battered yet stay silent,[37] but it would be in everyone's interest to know the figure. Not that the fact of victims exonerates the perpetrators of the same sex, but because men and women are not so different that they must be classified into two heterogeneous categories. Whatever their sex, the violent ones – even if much more numerous among men – show a lack of adjustment, some might say a malevolence, that owes something to the pathological. Suffering from serious psychological problems that worsen under the effects of alcohol or drugs, they can in no circumstances represent the norm, even if the pathological is never very far from the normal.

Men and women are subject to this pathology because violence belongs to humanity. We learn to channel it with greater or lesser success, but there is no lack of opportunity for frustration and conflict, and in such circumstances our obedience to prohibitions is sorely tested. Violence escapes our control, at worst through acts, at best through words.

However, the great majority of the women and men in this country live together, and separate from each other, in a civilized manner. Not without pain or conflict, but without violence. If a regulation of conflict belongs to a policed humanity, male and female, it is, on the other hand, a dangerous utopia to believe that it is possible to eradicate it. In a relationship, whether same sex or opposite sex, there cannot be an economy of tension or psychological pressure. According to circumstances, the tensions or pressures will either be buried in silence, or brought to light with all the risk of the excesses associated with anger. But to try to censure verbal violence by assimilating it to physical violence is to make a bad calculation. Whatever one might say, to wound with words is something of a different nature than to wound with blows. It is a weapon that both sexes can dispose of equally and which sometimes deflects the use of physical violence.

To impose silence on the injustice of words is to forbid the expression of anger. It is possible, of course, to dream of a gentle and controlled humanity that has gone so far as to forget the very meaning of this barbarous word; but until then, the verbal duel or a good row remains in many cases the best way of soothing tensions and putting an end to conflict. Either by surmounting the conflict or by understanding that it is insurmountable.

The abuse of power

Traditionally the 'abuse of power' as an expression is applied to men. Possessing all the power, financial, political, moral, religious – not to mention physical power – they have often used and abused it to the point of tyranny. In the world of politics, democracy and the balance of power have been invented, limiting abuse, without eradicating it entirely. In a relationship, power sharing is a much more delicate matter, because there democracy rests above all on love and respect for the other. However, in fifty years, the Western couple has made much progress. Since women have entered the work-force in large numbers, they have given themselves the means of acquiring an independence unknown to their mothers. Even where, for the more fragile among them, this independence is very relative, work is as indispensable for a woman as it is for a man. From the moment she can survive without him, she also possesses the atomic bomb that is separation or divorce.

However, financial autonomy does not resolve all the power issues. Other, more subtle forms of dependence exist, more secret ones that are perhaps more difficult to surmount. One example is sexual, emotional or psychological dependence. In this case, the one holds the upper hand over the other and imagines being able to impose his or her rules and whims without risk of retaliation. Contrary to what one might believe, this psychological power is not in essence male, and neither is its abuse. According to the relationship, it is either he or she who dominates, he or she who is in a state of dependence.

If emotional blackmail, insults and psychological pressure were to be taken into account among the global indicators of domestic violence, it would be an easy matter to put the Enveff questionnaire (see p. 13 above) to a representative sample of 7,000 men from twenty to fifty-nine, as was previously done for women. It would not only be more equitable, but it would give a different idea of domestic violence, and also a fairer idea of men and women. To give the impression that only men are jealous, badly behaved and tyrannical is an absurdity that should urgently be challenged.

Finally, there exists another kind of abuse of power that remains shrouded in secrecy. For thirty years, women have held undivided power over procreation. If it now appears to be absolutely legitimate for the woman to decide, in the last resort, whether she should go through with a pregnancy or not, it is, on the other hand, an abuse of power to make use of the sperm of a man who does not want a child. That a man can no longer procreate carelessly or against a woman's will is considerable progress, but it is morally wrong to impose paternity on someone who has explicitly rejected it. These abuses of power can hardly be the object of surveys or statistics. Everything takes place in the secrecy of individual consciences, in the context of a tête-à-tête or denial on one side and the other. Some will think that it is only a fair reversal of fortune after five thousand years of men's absolute rule over the bellies of women. Others will say that it would be enough to provide male contraception to avoid that kind of inconvenience. Or finally, that a woman has indeed the right to produce a child if she asks nothing else from the progenitor. Nevertheless, at a time when we are trying to develop a sense of paternal responsibility, it seems at the very least contradictory to bypass the will of the other and to use him for a purpose he takes exception to.

When feminists alert the authorities to violence against women it is their duty and it does them honour. When experts in the social sciences bring to light behaviour patterns that are little known, or not known at all, it is their job. But omission and silence is never neutral. To recognize the existence of female violence in no way minimizes the import of male violence and the urgency of the need to contain it and to help its victims. But in order to better fight against our weaknesses, whether natural or the product of education, we must renounce the angelic vision of women which accompanies the demonization of men.

In wanting to systematically ignore the violence and the power of women,[38] to proclaim them constantly oppressed, therefore innocent, a portrait in reverse is being drawn of a humanity split in half and bearing little resemblance to the truth. On the one side are the victims of male oppression, on the other side the all-powerful tormentors. To combat this situation, more and more feminist voices are attacking male sexuality identified as the root of evil. In so doing, they are tracing the contours of a female sexuality that contradicts the way mores have evolved, and redefine a 'female nature' we thought had been forgotten.

3
Contradiction

Increasingly we are surrounded by a double sexual obsession. On the one hand, repetitive slogans remind us that we are under an obligation to reach orgasm, inappropriately called 'being fulfilled'. On the other hand, there is a reminder of female dignity, sullied by undesired sexual attention, the scope of which is being constantly widened and redefined. On the one hand, since the 1970s everything is being done to take morality out of sex and to push ever further the limits of what constitutes transgression; on the other hand, the notion of sexual sacrilege is being reinvented. Object of consumption or sacred object, playful activity or criterion of dignity, sex has become the object of two discourses that are opposed almost word for word, and it is what is chiefly at stake in the new moral feminism.

By resacralizing sexuality, the second wave of feminism has radically turned away from the libertarian feminism that preceded it. In an osmosis with the demands of 1968, that discourse had declared loud and clear its wish to blow up the very foundation of patriarchy, men's mastery of women's sexuality. The great battle for the right to contraception and abortion was waged as much in order to reclaim power over procreation as it was for obtaining new sexual freedoms. 'A mother, if I choose to be' also meant 'enjoy sex without any limits'. And so the first wave of feminism not only largely contributed to the liberation of women, but also to the trivialization of sexuality.

Hardly were these new freedoms conquered than a disapproving growl could be heard coming from the other side of the Atlantic. It was the voices of radical lesbian feminists who denounced this trivialization, which was, according to them, all to the advantage of men and to the detriment of women. By believing that they could liberate themselves from the male yoke, it seemed that libertarian feminists had, on the contrary, contributed to its reinforcement. More than ever, women were taking on the role of disposable objects. Female humiliation was at its peak. Correspondingly, the nature of male and female sexuality was being questioned. The former, out of control, violent, conquering. The latter, more tender, delicate and faithful. Some came to the conclusion that the two sexes were incompatible; others, more numerous, claimed that the brake had to be put on a trivialization of sex which incited male violence. Little by little, the idea insinuated itself into people's minds that the female sex was indeed a sanctuary and that there was only one kind of female sexuality. The so-called liberated ones, those who considered a good fuck to be no more important than a good meal, became the exceptions to the rule. They were supposed to be virilized women, and therefore alienated, the unhappiest of the lot being without any contest the prostitutes who dared to call themselves free. Not only were they contributing to the vulgarization of the image and the body of woman (just like the striptease artist, the porn star, the bimbo or the model turned into a sex object to help sell mustard), but they also betrayed their enslaved sisters, victims of the worst kind of Mafiosi pimps. After the critique of sex as consumption, it was the turn of the commercialization of sex. In less time than it takes to say it, that kind of feminism once more found the moralizing accents of the old Judeo-Christianity and participated in a renaissance of the sexual stereotypes that had been so hard to shed.

To the predatory man who thinks only of his pleasure was

juxtaposed his victim who thinks only of love. Terrorized by the dominating male, she no longer dares to or no longer knows how to say *no*. However, she never ceases to be reminded of the fact that sexuality is a danger zone where she risks leaving her integrity and her dignity. Curiously, there is a silence about those women who say *yes* and merrily line up their male conquests. People avoid commenting in any way on the autobiographical work of Catherine Millet,[1] no doubt for fear of appearing puritanical, but don't hesitate to take to the streets, as did the Chiennes de Garde,[2] in protest against the restriction of the film *Baise-moi* to the over-eighteens. It is true that this film tells the story of the criminal romp of two women who kill all those who cross their path in revenge for their terrible life. It was perhaps not a bad idea to show men, through the inversion of roles, the horror of their own violence. For once that they were in the role of victims, the pedagogical advantage was perhaps worth offending our sensibilities for. Two women in the throes of sadism could only be an academic hypothesis, or else creatures crazed by the horrible way they had been treated.[3]

For all that, it is very rare for a feminist from any side of the spectrum to call for violence in response to violence. The form of struggle chosen is always the democratic, and therefore the legitimate one. It proceeds in three stages: the moral awareness of the violence committed against women, its criminalization, followed by the recourse to the courts. In other words, the ideological battle is fundamental. But in fighting today for the extension of the definition of the sexual offence to prostitution and pornography, politically correct feminism, draped in its offended dignity, unhesitatingly allies itself with the most traditional moral order. Its acknowledged enemy is the execrable consumer society, the expression of an offending liberal capitalism; the enemy is also libertarian feminism, accused of being its blind accomplice. There is something fundamental at stake in the battle now being waged. What is involved is none other than a redefinition of the relationship between men and women and of their reciprocal freedoms.

Sexual reality

The image is omnipresent. No one is unaware, not even young children, that sex is everywhere, crudely exhibited in the cinemas, on television, in advertising, magazines, literature or private conversations. As Xavier Deleu rightly says, 'A sexual cacophony leads to the saturation of the public space by the accumulation of erotic signs.'[4] The aims on the banner: putting an end to two thousand years of collective repression and private frustration. Today, the lifting of taboos is a rallying call which is not to be trifled with. The least reticence in the face of this New Sexual Order[5] and you run the risk of playing the bad part of the censor, the tight-arse, in short, someone very old-fashioned. Here is not the place for picking apart this constraining new order. Others have already done so with great talent.[6] Rather, the aim is to start to grasp the distance that lies between today's sexual reality and the new feminist morality.

The end of norms

In order to give us the flavour of the sexual order that presides over male domination in traditional societies (in this instance the Baruya of New Guinea or the Kabyles of North Africa), Michel Bozon sums it up in a single sentence: 'Man gives orders and rides the woman.'[7] To note that we are light years away from that model is something of an understatement. The opposite has even become the sexual configuration that is *de rigueur* in contemporary cinema. But the end of norms does not stop there. Autobiographies of young people, surveys on sexual habits and other kinds of works on various minority practices display a new unbridled and multiform sexuality. Some see it as a manifestation of appeasement and liberation, others see it as having no heart or soul, others finally, as the locus of all violence and a refound savagery.

To read the women's literature of these last years,[8] young girls drop their knickers with an ease that confounds the older generation. Curiosity, desire, pride, provocation or will to

ot quite clear just what is the driving force of
But one thing for sure is that virginity at eight-
lot more worry than pride. Believing that you
nsumed by psychological problems calls for
measures: recourse to a shrink or a 'deflowering'
that ... s very little desire. The first step accomplished,
there remains for the explorers of sex, for those hungry for
strong sensations, an assortment of practices to test or to
adopt. Not dying an idiot – or innocent – seems to have
become a preoccupation the two sexes share more and more.

Two surveys of the sexual habits of the French, conducted
ten years apart, give some measure of insight into the way
behaviour has evolved and how far the norms of the past have
been cast aside. The first is a quantitative study of a sample of
20,000 people interviewed by telephone in the course of
1991–2.[9] It was possible to find that – in comparison with the
previous 1972 study by Professor Simon – fellatio and cunni-
lingus have become common practices (90 per cent), that
women masturbate more than they did twenty years ago, that
24 per cent of women have experimented with anal penetration (against 30 per cent of heterosexual men),[10] but that
only 3 per cent of men and women said they practised it
often.

Viewing pornographic magazines or films was an emi-
nently male activity (more that 50 per cent of the men
between eighteen and forty, against 30 per cent of the
women). Finally, among the 'fairly rare' sexual activities was
the use of personal ads for the purpose of sex (less than 20
per cent of thirty-five year old men), and among the 'rare'
ones were threesomes, swinging and the use of an object to
obtain sexual excitement. There was no mention of the more
extreme practices, from sado-masochism, to fist-fucking and
the gang-bang.

In 2002, the qualitative study conducted by Janine
Mossuz-Lavau conducted among seventy men and women
from all social backgrounds and of all ages, with the help of
in-depth interviews, proved the 'extraordinary diversity in
the attitudes to sex existing in individuals living at the same

time in the same country'.[11] The lesson to be drawn from this is that 'in this domain, there is no conception of the norm'. To the extent that in an interview with her a journalist from *Libération* observes that 'we have the impression that people with a classical or conventional sexuality, who do not swing or go in for threesomes, have become rare birds indeed'.[12] In reality, Janine Mossuz-Lavau's work shows a whole range of behaviour patterns, from women who have been leading a very rich sex life with the same man for the last twenty years to others who have nothing to envy Catherine Millet for. We learn that young women practise sodomy more than before, even if they do so less than boys, that young girls have a more egalitarian conception of sex and reject the old stereotypes. 'What has changed is that women have become more demanding. They have got it into their head that they have a right to pleasure [. . .] I have a lot of statements', says J. Mossuz-Lavau, 'from women who have dumped men because they didn't make them come. One of them told me that she kicked a boyfriend out in the middle of the night, because she wasn't "getting anything from him". This kind of behaviour is quite new.'[13]

What has also changed is that men and women need to explore their fantasies and there are many more people out there than we might think who enjoy practices that might be called 'marginal'.[14]

Does this mean that everybody in France has sex without any qualms? 'I have not encountered a France that is frustrated or unhappy,' the author answers, 'there is a great freedom in France, and something of the order of play and joy.'[15]

Not everyone shares this optimism. To begin with, there are many written accounts that bear witness to a trashy kind of sexuality, sometimes astonishingly violent, in which relationships of domination and submission prevail. In such cases, the body is merely a receptacle to be exploited, sometimes to the point of destruction. It is simply an object of consumption. Without going to these extremes, others note that 'hard-core' pornography is more and more invasive in advertisements, videos and films, that it 'penetrates collective consciousness', that the X-rated film now serves as 'the original matrix of fantasies'.[16] At twelve, three-quarters of boys, and half the girls have already seen a pornographic film.[17] They discover the crudeness of words (fist-fucking, strap-on dildos, triple penetration), the brutality of acts and the representation of the body-machine. If they had access to hard-core stuff, they might have witnessed group rape (gang-bang), a category that is apparently very much in demand in sex shops, and all the exploits that a torturer can inflict on the body of a woman.

Even if pornographic representations are aimed only at fantasy and sexual excitement, we are forced to agree with J. Mossuz-Lavau that more and more people need to live out their fantasies. The numerous articles devoted to marginal, even extreme sexual practices, personal ads in even the most mainstream magazines, and especially sexual offerings on the internet have turned banal what only yesterday was considered abnormal or immoral. Erotic salons have multiplied during the last ten years, along with swinging clubs for swapping partners or hard-core private parties. Even if they are only the province of a tiny minority, society's outlook on these very particular pleasures has changed. As the sociologist Véronique Poutrain observes,

> sado-masochistic practices, grouped under the banner BDSM,[18] if not a recent phenomenon, are more visible today, and are gradually becoming normalized. They infiltrate the universe of sex generally and nowadays benefit from a structured commercial network. Whether they attract or repulse, from now on they are part of the public sphere. If specialized boutiques such as Démonia exist, it is also true that there is no longer any sex shop without its S&M department [. . .] [These practices] are no longer reserved for devotees in the know: sadomasochism has also become something that 'colours', gives an orgasmic intensity and something that 'excites' the whole world of images.[19]

The author remarks that the perception of sado-masochism has evolved 'until it ends up being defined as a playful recreational sexuality, accessible to all. Nowadays, magazines aimed at the age range of fifteen to twenty-five do not hesitate to present these practices as no longer a pathology, but as a rich and amusing sexual entertainment providing new pleasures.'

The same observation holds true for swinging. The sociologist Daniel Welzer-Lang, writing in the context of his work on male domination and different forms of prostitution, has devoted four years of ethnographic research to what he calls 'the swinger's planet'. Using sources ranging from specialized publications to personal ads and their replies, from fifty interviews with the men and women inhabiting that planet to *in situ* observation of the nudist colony of Cap d'Agde and other meeting places, Welzer-Lang and his team offer the best possible insight into the people who enjoy such practices.[20]

What this study immediately shows us is the spread of these practices in the second half of the 1990s. To give an indication: the increase in the number of commercial swinging places in a city like Lyon (from 9 in 1992 to more than 20 in 1996) and that of specialist personal ads (from 800 in 1993 in the main swingers' magazine to 2,500 in 2001). The number of swingers is estimated to be between 300,000 and 400,000 people. They are mainly men: 51 per cent men on their own, 41 per cent couples (so about 75 per cent men); 3.5 per cent are women on their own, and the rest is made up of transvestites and diverse other groups. The areas densely populated with swingers are the Île de France, the Rhone Valley and the South of France, but adepts do not hesitate to travel hundreds of kilometres to meet up or attend special evenings in clubs. D. Welzer-Lang remarks that the spread of these practices is a European phenomenon that involves a great variety of punters:

> The greatest proportion of these meeting places are for people over forty [...]. However, there is a parallel phenomenon emerging among a significant minority of young people between twenty and thirty-five [...] In the afternoons, the admittance fee to the clubs is only a drink from the bar, and this allows access for clients of more modest means, even if the presence of

working-class men or of women remains small; the evenings are for couples, cost substantially more and are mainly frequented by the middle or upper classes; as for 'private parties', they are generally reserved for the upper classes.

Even if this phenomenon only affects a small minority of French men (4 per cent) and French women (1 per cent), it is undemonized by the media. 'Sexual modernity obliges us to go into a swinger's club at least once, "just to see".'[21] Nothing can be more revealing in this respect than a television programme broadcast one evening in 2001 at prime time on a national television channel during which young couples calmly told of their experiences of swinging and the ways in which this was beneficial to their relationship. It is not a coincidence that Michel Houellebecq shows his heroes – or rather his antiheroes, since they are such caricatures of the middle classes – as vacationing in Cap-d'Agde and frequenting S&M bars, on the look-out for a kind of sexual excitement that goes beyond the everyday.[22] From now on, anything that spices up desire is welcome, even if extreme sexual practices such as hard-core S&M or gang-bangs remain in the public imagination the privilege or the sign of the perversion of a tiny minority.

Body-object or sex-machine

In our society where sexual consumption rules, the body must be young, ready to perform and exciting. To arrive at this ideal, there are few sacrifices that women in particular do not agree to make. From the most benign to the most painful, bodily modifications mean that the body is to be approached like an object to be moulded according to current fashion and the passage of time. Men are obsessed by its performance, women by its appearance. These obsessions are magnified by the erotico-pornographic images that assail us.

Without even considering the problem of hair, especially pubic hair, which calls for the torment of 'bikini' wax, or the terror of cellulite and superfluous fat that is fought with the help of draconian diets and liposuction, Western women increasingly resort to the rituals of plastic surgery. Apart from the classic operations of the face-lift and the nose job, they seek breast implants to increase the size of their bust, or on the contrary undergo surgery to reduce it, change the contours of their buttocks and their thighs, and even their nipples, or their genital organs if they do not like their shape. The whole of the female body, even genitals, is potentially subject to modification. For all that, it would be wrong to think that the male body is altogether able to escape this torment of perfectionism. According to plastic surgeons, more and more men are getting face-lifts (one in four or five operations) or imposing strict dietary restrictions on themselves.

In the younger generation, the practices of piercing and tattooing are more evenly split between the two sexes, involving simultaneously a wish to personalize and adorn the body and an erotic preoccupation. It is said that the piercing of sexual organs has an exciting function, like a tongue stimulating the base of the penis during fellatio.

The body is treated like an object that is manipulated and tortured in every possible way. It is also divested of its erotic characteristics in favour of some of its parts. Dominique Folscheid rightly observes:

> The more we enter into a pure logic of sex, the more we become a captive of its mechanistic demands, the more bodies must be disinvested, the more they must be split into pieces and dispersed in order to turn their sexually strategic parts into instruments and toys. It is only within particular zones of the body, said to be erotogenic, that sex perceives a space of excitement.[23]

This is perfectly illustrated by pornographic imagery that cuts up bodies all the better to show the genitals or their details in close-up. Some back-room practices do so as well, and if Houellebecq is to be believed, they are no longer the preserve of homosexuals.

The splitting up and the instrumentalization of the body no longer applies only to marginal sexualities or only to men.

The new fashion for sex toys aimed at women is one indication of this. In New York, London or Paris, stylish new sex shops have opened for a mainly female clientele. All the objects that elicit pleasure can be found there. The opening of an erotic department in a Sonia Rykiel shop gave rise to many articles in the press, all of the same voice. After the description of the candy-coloured fluorescent dildos, of the Rabbit that created a sensation in the cult American television series *Sex and the City*, the novelty is justified with these magic words: removing guilt from female pleasure. Nathalie Rykiel speaks of humour, dedramatization and performance. 'Contrary to English boutiques which sell beautiful but inefficient objects, I have chosen to select objects that give real pleasure. When you take this kind of path, you have to follow it till the end. Above all, you must not be hypocritical! Our sex toys are certainly pretty and playful, but mostly, they work!'[24]

Success was waiting in the wings. In just a few weeks, *Elle* points out, the house sold hundreds of erotic items, and the waiting lists were overflowing. From that point, the right to solitary and mechanical pleasures became democratized at high speed. The mail order catalogue *3 Suisses* offers raffish gadgets to its clientele,[25] and electronic commerce is no less successful. All the objects you dream of but are afraid to buy in a sex shop can be ordered from home. There, too, the talk is of the way guilt can be shed, and the owner of one of these sites confides to *Libération* that it receives between 150 and 200 orders each day, that women buyers account for 40 per cent of the sale of these gadgets, and finally that, three years after its launch, he expects turnover to reach 2.3 million euros in 2002, that is, double the previous year.[26]

Solitary pleasures, mechanical enjoyment, Boris Cyrulnik is not wrong to note that we need each other less and less: 'With this mechanization of sex, men are at risk of becoming nothing more for women than dildos or baby-planters.'[27] At the very least, machines that have to perform at least as well as the ones that can be bought in a shop. Under these circumstances, men's anxiety about impotence, and their resort to a whole chemical panoply in order to be equal to the challenge are understandable.

Women are well on their way to getting rid of guilt. Waves of media attention and the trivialization of pornography have already produced their effects on the younger ones. Some dream of becoming porn stars like Tabatha Cash, Mélanie Coste or Ovidie. The idols of prepubescent girls are the stars of the videos that are constantly being shown on the cable music channels. Performers like Britney Spears and Christina Aguilera can be seen 'exhibiting themselves, lasciviously rubbing up against well-endowed males, and playing with the symbols of S&M'.[28] Even if these are the fantasies of the men who produce these videos and not the dreams of the young female viewers, girls are still confronted from very early on with the image of a mechanized and brutal sexuality.

Liberation from taboos or the tyranny of fantasy? Dedramatization or the reduction of sexuality to physical sensation? Legitimation of desire or the unleashing of violence? Personal flowering or solitude and sexual misery? Trapped between those nostalgic for the past and the partisans of going ever further, the majority asks itself what the right road is to follow. This is not the case for the new moral feminism, sure of its analysis and of the changes that must be made.

The myth of a domesticated sexuality

The diagnosis is obvious. Since the beginning of time, it is men who have imposed their kind of sexuality on women. The sexual pseudo-liberation that we are witnessing has multiplied its effects. These are domination and violence. From pornography to conjugal rape, from gang rape in the suburbs to prostitution, we seem to be witnessing an unleashing of male sexuality without any limits. It is high time to invert the deal and trace the contours of a different kind of sexuality, one that would be free from the infernal relationship of domination and submission, the power of money and the obscure ambiguities of desire. A transparent sexuality, democratic and contractual. A gentle and innocent sexuality that demands a community between fantasies and perversions, an identity of drives and their domestication. In sum, a single sexuality that posits a resemblance between the sexes at the point where in fact it does not exist.

'The fairy tale of purity'

Victim feminism that only thinks in terms of 'male domination' formally defends itself from any puritanical or moralizing intension. There is no question of forbidding sex or of locking it into the sphere of marriage, something that would make no sense today. However, the notions of licit and illicit sex have reappeared on the occasion of recent debates on prostitution. Even though prohibitionists and abolitionists of all kinds are more vocal about what they condemn than about what they preach, it is not difficult to perceive what good sexuality would look like.[29]

The absolute vice is money, which objectifies the female body and dehumanizes woman in preparation for her sexual and social domination.[30] In the double lineage of Christianity and Marxism, money is the expression of corruption and the means for the brutal domination of one person by the other. A differentiation is no longer made between the sale of an organ and a sexual transaction, rape and prostitution, voluntary prostitution and sexual slavery. They are all spoken of as the mercantilization of the body and the infringement of human rights. The only kind of sex that is permitted is free, and therefore innocent, and desire must be reciprocal.

Two little texts give a clearer idea of what a good sexuality is supposed to be like. The first one is an excerpt from a Quebec manifesto against prostitution. Having denounced those who 'accept socially that there are human beings who are constrained to serve the *pathological* desires of certain men – for it is indeed a pathology, since paying for a prostitute means wanting to fuck someone who doesn't want you', the author indicates what she understands to be a normal, healthy sexuality: 'In a healthy society, still unfortunately a utopia, people would make love only to share *tenderness* and a *common desire*. The mutual pleasure of the two partners would be the only possible way of approaching sex. Most religions have separated spirituality and sexuality, even though the latter should also have been thought of in terms of the quests of the soul.'[31]

This idea of a 'happy and healthy' sexuality is also put forward in a petition led by Florence Montreynaud, ex-president of the Chiennes de Garde, today head of La Meute [the Pack].[32] Dated 29 July 2000, she has entitled the text: 'Vive l'amour libre et gratuit [In praise of love that is free and for free] and calls for the abolition of prostitution. Not inclined towards repression, F. Montreynaud pleads for the education of those she calls machos, and whom she would later qualify as *viandards* [sexual carnivores]. The problem with machos, she says, is often that they separate love from desire.[33] This is a revealing statement: good sex can only be conceived, in fact, within love, or shared desire. Drive-led sex, which disregards emotion, is outside the law, it is amoral and so should be fought. It is even associated with rape by many feminist associations.

This conception of a sexuality presented as the only one with any legitimacy comes up against many difficulties and gives rise to many questions. First of all, drive-led and financially transacted sex is not the sole domain of machos and *viandards*. There are more women who resort to buying sex than is generally admitted.[34] And perhaps these would number even more if the last taboos that still restrict female sexuality were lifted. A woman claiming the same sexual freedom as a man, that is to say, separate from any kind of feeling, is still considered to be either corrupt or an exception to the rule. Should the male prostitute whose services she buys be considered a rape victim? Is pleasure for pleasure's sake still to be equated with sin as it was in the past? On the other hand, the identification of the client with a rapist in the eyes of the law or to a *viandard* involves the worst kind of stigmatization of the prostitute (whether male or female), who is thus deprived of any dignity and responsibility. Understood as the ultimate degree of degradation, the activity that prostitutes engage in reduces them to the level of 'absolute victim', a member of an 'underclass' and, even more insulting, to the level of 'meat'. Contempt shows through the flood of compassion, all the more inexcusable since it emanates from women who sincerely believe that they are feminists and at the forefront of the battle for equality between the sexes.

Finally, this conception of an 'innocent' sexuality that excludes any venality poses a problem that is carefully avoided. Where does vice begin and end? If freedom from monetary considerations and a reciprocity in desire are the criteria that we keep for a virtuous sexuality, what is one to make of men and women who choose their partner according to their social status or financial standing? What can be said of those who go to bed without desire, who do it either as a good turn for someone, or in exchange for something? What to think of this recent survey by the marketing intelligence agency IFOP according to which 96 per cent of French men state that money is needed in order to seduce, and 28 per cent agree that offering a weekend abroad 'works every time'?[35] Some would see this as one of the perverse effects of the ultra-liberalism that is to be fought, others as the end of romance and the dissociation between love and sex. But the feminists who are holding out for purity don't see it this way. Since mentalities cannot be changed, street prostitution can always be a good target. As always the fairy tale of purity is concluded by a show of repression. Right and left alike, the municipality of Bordeaux or the municipality of Paris demand that the sinful couple be punished, or alternatively, only the client, which is a roundabout way of punishing the prostitute, by taking away her livelihood. In the 'feminist' camp of the municipality of Paris, everything is planned: a two-year jail sentence (four times longer than in Sweden!) and a 30,000 euro fine followed by community service for the recalcitrant client.[36] On the other hand, we merrily medicalize as well as punish. These clients are sick and should be submitted to an 'injunction of care'. As for the prostitutes, we serendipitously learn that they are suffering from considerable psychological dysfunctions and specifically from the syndrome of 'decorporalization'.[37] In short, everything is arranged so that war can be waged against the nasty drives.

Transparency and consent

The two terms of transparency and consent go together. Consenting to the sexual act implies a clarity and neatness in the demand. Everything must be explicitly stated. As in certain Protestant countries of old, there are to be no curtains on the windows. Nothing in our deepest selves can remain hidden. Desire should be shown naked, visible to the other down to its last curve. Little attention is given to the modesty that tries to hide the crudity or brutality of some of its aspects. Every facet of ourselves must be talked about and shown. In this sense, the theoreticians of consent link up with the same spirit that informs both the confession manuals of the sixteenth and seventeenth centuries, and the young exhibitionist literature of today. We recall that in the former, a long list of questions about sexuality was drawn up for the benefit of the confessor in order to ensure that he should forget nothing and could measure all the more efficiently the seriousness of the penitent's sin: 'Did he put his hand here? There? Has he entered through this orifice or that? Did he come inside or outside?' And so on. Today, confession is no longer wrested but is freely bestowed in front of the widest possible public. Girls and boys are afflicted with a kind of exhibitionist prurience and do not hesitate to display their most intimate desires and the misfortunes of their sex. From the famous writer to the most obscure punter facing the television cameras, everybody dreams only of openly displaying all of the vicissitudes of their sex lives. The tête-à-tête with the confessor or the psychoanalyst shows its limitations and its dullness. But the objective remains the same: to tell everything, to unveil everything.

The feminist vision does not share in any way this desire

for publicity. But the exigencies of a consent devoid of any ambiguity calls for desire to have the same degree of explicitness. The goal is to preserve a full and undivided freedom in the face of the other's desire. 'To give in does not mean to consent',[38] we have been taught. And on all American campuses the fact that the least psychological pressure brings an immediate lack of legitimacy to sexuality is repeated to satiety. It is just another way to speak of rape. It leads to the significance of words becoming extremely important. The feminist gloss is inexhaustible on the topic of the 'no' or the 'yes'. Strangely, only two cases in four are envisaged. The 'no that means no' and the 'yes that means no'. No one is interested in the 'yes that means yes', and even less in the 'no that means yes'.

On campus, no is always taken to mean no. And in fact, when a sexual proposition is unwanted, you are expected to let it be known without any ambiguity. The male predator can pretend not to hear or exert different kinds of pressures on his prey. If the pressure is physical, if he uses force, without a doubt this constitutes rape. But in the eyes of the theoreticians of consent, psychological pressures are no less constraining. They derive from what is called 'non-violent sexual coercion'.[39] Verbal coercion is defined in the following way: 'woman's consent to an unwanted sexual activity because of the man's use of verbal arguments not including verbal threats of force.' For example, he could threaten to put an end to their relationship if she does not make love; he could tell her that she is frigid or else that everybody else is doing it. If she submits to his arguments, it is a yes that means no. She has given in but not consented and we are back to the problematic of rape.

At the end of the 1980s a Harvard student wrote a play about rape, *Calling it Rape*, as a pedagogical exercise. The goal was to alert colleagues about rape founded on verbal misunderstanding. Katie Roiphe describes a passage:

The boy and girl are watching videos and he starts to come on to her. The girl does not want to have sex. As the situation progresses, she says, in an oblique effort to communicate her lack of enthusiasm, 'if you are going to fuck me, use a condom.' He interprets that as a yes, but it's really a no. And according to this play, what happens next, condom or no condom, is rape.[40]

So words are not enough to legitimate a sexual act. Beyond words, there is a need to assess intentions that are not formulated, repulsions that are not admitted to and all the difficulties inherent in a woman's 'no'. Female passivity and timidity that we were wrong to relegate to the past must be taken into account. By the strength of such a doctrine, a woman's 'yes' should therefore be subject to caution, unless it is called out loud and clear. As Michel Feher says, there is always 'a measure of doubt pertaining to the validity of the consent that a woman grants her seducer'.[41]

Strangely, this taking into account of woman's timidity or of her hidden intentions is rarely envisaged in the inverse situation: the no that means yes. Eric Fassin, willing spokesman for American feminism, admits that 'it is not rare that a woman responds with a symbolic refusal and resistance for the form of it, all the more to signify her assent', but he only sees in this the remainder of Victorian times.[42] Patrick Hochart and Claude Habib, on the contrary, in their rereading of book V of Rousseau's *Émile*, refer us back to the lack of symmetry in sexual roles and to the complementarity of male and female desire.[43] Perhaps it is inscribed in nature that man 'conquers' and that woman 'cedes' to a tender violence. These are words obviously incompatible with a feminist point of view since they leave the door open for all manner of abuse.

However, if we admit that a woman can say yes while thinking no, the reverse should also be acknowledged – unless we eliminate the word 'modesty' once and for all from our vocabulary, as the signifier of a feeling or of a hypocrisy that is no longer relevant. But is this really the case? Not unless we also think that the heart and the body are always in step and that we stay to the last detail in mastery of our desires. But the theory of consent has no stake in such trifles. It demands that right at the start we draw up a complete catalogue of our wants and our aversions. Which brings us to the idea of the sexual contract.

Consent and contract

In the early 1990s, to much amusement in France, but also in the United States, Antioch College, Ohio, proposed a charter aiming to regulate the sexual act. Sex had to be the object of a detailed agreement between the two parties, covering all stages of the process. This implies asking and obtaining permission for the smallest gesture of sexual intimacy. Ideally, it would have been a written contract – before a notary, why not? – in order to avoid *a posteriori* litigation.

Even among the most convinced feminists this sexual contract appeared as an aberrant caricature of the idea of reciprocal consent. Sex that no longer leaves any place for imagination and spontaneity signals well and truly the end of eroticism. As some have remarked: 'The probability of two lovers marching completely in step towards the free and equal exchange that alone legitimates their frolics [. . .] to see their natural desires awaken and ripen at exactly the same moment and at the same rate is obviously very small.'[44] However, this absurd contract is the logical consequence of the transparency the theory of consent demands. If unwanted sexual attention amounts to harassment, and if the ambiguity of words and gestures can give rise to legal action, and if, contrary to the adage, the person who says nothing does not consent, some sort of preliminary contract has to be established one way or another. The game of the unsaid, of surprises, of masks and initiatives no longer has its place in 'legal' sex.

This is why some American feminists, more articulate or dogmatic than others, have suggested that the contractual formula be made into the norm of heterosexual relations. In a short essay that won a prize from the American Philosophical Association in 1992, the philosopher Loïs Pineau developed a model for something she calls *communi-*

cative sex, inspired by the rules of Antioch College. In her eyes, the advantage of such a system is that no man could argue any more that a no can also mean yes: the number of rapes, and in particular date rapes, would diminish considerably. As Daphne Patai remarks, Loïs Pineau, in contrast to Catharine MacKinnon, suggests that women are completely capable of giving explicit and verbal consent without remaining in the realm of gestures and innuendo.[45] Not only is explanation not a problem, but it is a must.

In France, the theme of the sexual contract has never been approached in these terms. People are content to say that 'consent is a nice word, and a good thing',[46] while keeping well away from defining what that 'thing' is. Certainly, everybody understands what the withholding of consent means, as well as its opposite, sexual compulsion. But we know very well that consent in the sphere of love and sex is often played out in the spaces in-between: in the maybe, in indecision, in the simultaneous yes and no. We do not know what to say about this complex, often contradictory grey area, and prefer to ignore it. The unconscious no longer has a place in feminist theory and politics. It is the price to pay for the exigencies of transparency.

The only instance of a known sexual contract is the one that defines the act of prostitution. However, it is something that abolitionist feminists condemn. But in this case there actually exists a preliminary agreement between the two parties about the gestures and acts to be willingly bestowed and those to be refused. Each gesture and act has its price and the independent prostitute can accept or refuse the demands of the client. Transparency is complete because modesty and feeling are excluded. Paradoxically, it is for this very reason that the contract is void. In the eyes of the abolitionists, there can be no free consent to sex that is situated from the outset outside emotion or desire. To turn your body into an object of transactions is a sign of slavery and therefore of alienation. We are told that no sane woman can 'sink' into prostitution by choice. Only economic misery, physical constraint by a pimp and a heavily charged psychological past can explain such a situation. In this case, the consent of the prostitute means nothing and the sexual contract is void. So there should be no surprise that some people amalgamate rape and prostitution. 'The rape of women incontrovertibly uncovers the domination of men over women. It renders it visible. Prostitution makes possible the access to women's bodies with all the imaginary [*sic*] or real forms of violence that the client inflicts.'[47]

The model of female sexuality

The various studies on sexuality always make much of a distinction that is often drawn between male and female sexuality. To the question as to whether sex and emotion can be dissociated, men answer without any hesitation with the affirmative, but women do not. Even if, as Janine Mossuz-Lavau points out, sexual stereotypes are weakened and 'women are starting to behave like men and men are getting all touchy-feely', the idea of a distinction between male and female desire persists. During a debate between Pascal Bruckner and Paula Jacques on that theme, the former pointed out that 'male sexuality is simple, mechanical. Desire is all over the place, and if prostitution is exclusively for men [?] it is because male sexuality is a sexuality of immediate desire.' The latter also insists on the temporal differences and the archaic position of the male hunter. She thinks that there remains in women 'this curse that prevents them from having the prompt, volatile, unstable sexuality of men [. . .]. Can they only be moved if there is a feeling of love, in other words construction?'[48]

Even if Catherine Millet and her young sisters seem to escape the curse, sociological texts continue to underline the social but also the psychological differences between female and male desire. Michel Bozon notes that

> they do not have the same weight nor the same legitimacy in the sexual life of a couple. Asked as to who wanted it the most during their last sexual encounter, men and women both declared that

it was the woman in less than one case in ten, the man four or five times in ten, and the two in equal proportions the rest of the time. Women see male desire as dominant even more frequently than men do.[49]

Conscious of differences in the quality of desire according to gender, the market for pornographic films is starting to turn towards women. The initiative is from Denmark, where Lars von Trier has produced two X-rated films specifically conceived of as a response to female expectations. The director, Lisbeth Lynghoeft, explains that 90 per cent of pornographic films are produced by men for men and it is time to 'respond to the specific expectations of women in the area of eroticism and pornography. They want to see more preliminaries, bodies shown whole, and not reduced to genitals, narrative progression in the plot, the staging of credible characters with feelings. The only limitation imposed is respect for the woman: under no circumstance should she be violated or made to submit against her will.'[50]

'Preliminaries', 'length', 'feeling', this is the traditional triptych that defines female sexuality. 'Penetration', 'consumption', 'domination', the one that defines male sexuality. It is obviously this latter one that constitutes a problem for second wave feminists.

The denunciation of male sexuality

If it is thought that sex is the foundation of the oppression of women by men and that this explains their social inferiority, two possibilities can be envisaged according to whether an essentialist or culturalist philosophical perspective is adopted. In the first instance, the separation of the sexes is called for, along with a rejection of heterosexuality. In the second case, the transformation of male sexuality becomes the object of the struggle. Since the 1970s, American feminism has taken both these possibilities very far. But the repeated calls of separatist lesbian feminism to break with men have proved to be – no great surprise – unworkable. However much the philosopher

Joyce Trebilcot and a few others, as long ago as 1984, asked women to stop participating in the institution of heterosexuality, the injunction fell on deaf ears.[51] Culturalist discourse took over:

> Without renouncing their values, the guardians of female authenticity could then negotiate a movement of strategic retreat that would bring them to privilege a defensive and legislative use of the culture and sexuality they attribute to women. In other words, the second wave of cultural feminism, where the importance of legal experts (cf. C. MacKinnon) can be noted, tends to leave aside the question of compatibility between male and female sexualities in order to concentrate its efforts on the struggle against the abuses caused by male sexuality.[52]

If, officially, there is no longer any question of combating a male essence, but only its pathological manifestations (pornography, harassment, violence, prostitution, rape), the critique of masculinity is so radical and general that only a very small minority of men can hope perhaps to escape the anathema. To read A. Dworkin, C. MacKinnon or K. Barry, it is the sexuality of men in its entirety that is put in question, and alongside it, heterosexuality.

It is on the occasion of their fight against pornography that Dworkin and MacKinnon have developed their theory of the predatory and raping male.

First act: to re-establish the female point of view on sexuality:

> The point of view of men up to this time, called objective, has been to distinguish sharply between rape on the one hand and intercourse on the other; sexual harassment on the one hand and normal, ordinary sexual initiation on the other; pornography or obscenity on the one hand, and eroticism on the other. The male point of view defines them by distinction. What women experience does not so clearly distinguish the normal everyday things from abuse [. . .]. What we are saying is that sexuality in exactly these normal forms often does violate us. So long as we say that

these things are abuses of violence not sex [. . .] we leave the line between rape and intercourse, sexual harassment and sex roles, pornography and eroticism right where it is.[53]

C. MacKinnon expresses in the clearest possible terms her suspicion (or her certainty) that the most ordinary heterosexual act is actually rape. In the same article she reminds us that the juridical definition of rape implies penetration. 'And', she says, 'it is exactly what heterosexuality as a social institution is fixated around, the penetration of the penis into the vagina.'[54] Therefore, there is hardly any difference in kind between the two. But women are so alienated by the male point of view that defines them that they believe themselves to be free when they are not. Whoever may be their partner, lover, husband or rapist, women are always put in a position of submission or constraint.

Second case: the case against the penis. This time, it is Andrea Dworkin, who does not hide her homosexuality, who leads the charge against 'this piece of flesh, a few inches long'[55] responsible for male violence. In a repetitive and obsessional way, Dworkin develops the theme of an all-powerful, wounding and violent penis that is the very expression of masculinity.

Throughout male culture, the penis is seen as a weapon, specially a sword. The word 'vagina' means literally 'shield'. In a male supremacist society, reproduction takes on the same characteristic as a force, leading, at some point to death; the penis/sperm valued as potential agent of female death [*sic*]. For centuries, female dislike of sex, female frigidity, female avoidance of 'sex' have been legendary [. . .] this has been the silent rebellion of women against the force of the penis [. . .] The aversion of women for the penis and to sexuality as men define it must be seen not as puritanism, but as women's refusal to pay homage to the primary purveyor of male aggression, one on one, against women.[56]

Like her friend MacKinnon, and with even less caution, she concludes that rape is the paradigm of heterosexuality. At

least so long as the nature of masculinity has not been funda-
mentally changed.

The third act is yet to come: to police, soften, democratize
masculinity and the sexuality that expresses it. It is the only
way of exiting from the infernal opposition between the
predatory male and his powerless victim.

Policing male sexuality

If texts attacking male sexuality are becoming innumerable,
those clearly explaining what it should be are rare. Generally,
it is discernible in the spaces left by the critique. If all penetration is an aggression, the wished-for sexuality is that which
privileges caresses over the 'invasion of the vagina', to use
Dworkin's expression. In her eyes, sexuality separated from
the threat of rape that hovers over all heterosexual acts is
defined in four words: intimacy, tenderness, cooperation and
emotion.[57] As for Florence Montreynaud, who however
questions not her own heterosexuality but rather 'macho'
sexuality, she points out that 'the vocabulary of sex is so
impregnated with machismo that pleasures other than the
penetration of the vagina are called "preliminaries". To make
love is to "possess" or to "take" a woman. Seduction is seen like
a military operation, woman defending herself like a fortress
and the man "shooting his load", after which the party is
over.'[58]

It might be objected that the men who practise sex in such
a way only demonstrate their clumsiness and their ignorance.
They are bad lovers and not necessarily macho. On the other
hand, women are not inert objects with no will of their own.
Other than in cases of physical constraint – which constitute
rape – they are completely capable of saying if something
does not suit them and, in that case, of not renewing the
experience. Preliminaries are a matter of apprenticeship for
both sexes and do not necessarily have anything to do with
the four imperatives that define female sexuality according to
Dworkin.

Is Dworkin's not, in fact, a very partial vision of female sexuality? What would Catherine Millet and many others say about this very traditional model of female behaviour – even if it is a majority one? Without even considering a return to the pre-genital sexuality of children, as Andrea Dworkin advocates,[59] are we not hearing an injunction to 'feminize' male sexuality? Intimacy and tenderness are not the alpha and the omega of all desire. The violence of the drives is not exclusively male and does not necessarily end in rape. However, there is never any question of this. Nor of those women who have nothing in common with O, Pauline Réage's heroine, and who, without any complexes, look to having someone dominate them in bed, and having an 'associate' elsewhere.

The multiplicity of sexualities no longer needs to be proved. Neither does the complexity of the libido. However, the domestication of desire has not been completely given up. In this sense, we are indeed witnessing a return to a pre-Freudian state of things. It is true that in the nineteenth century there was indeed a question of channelling the libido within conjugal relations. Men and women were equally forbidden any enjoyment outside marriage (even if the prohibition was much more drastic for women than it was for men). Today, it is primarily male sexuality that is to be constrained. Not so much by forbidding any sexual relations with beings who are not responsible, such as children or the mentally ill, which is not something new,[60] but by redefining the nature of permissible sexuality. A number of surprising statements were made during debates on prostitution. One must 'put the brakes on the male drive', writes Françoise Héritier, who mistakes century and society when she denounces the sole 'permissibility' of that drive:

> One point is never discussed: it is the permissibility *exclusively* of the male drive, its need to be a legitimate component of man's nature, its right to express itself, all of which is denied to the female drive, down to its very existence [. . .]. The male drive is not to be tied down or interfered with, it can legitimately exert itself so long as it does not do so in a violent and brutal way.

Even though one might think that 1970s feminism has put an end precisely to this lack of symmetry, the author calls for a questioning of 'this apparently natural legitimacy of the male sex drive, not in order to totally repress it [?], which would not make sense, but to end up in an exercise that would recognize the parallel legitimacy of the female drive'.[61] The various reports on the sexual practices of the French show that the questioning has already taken place and the recalibration is under way. These are no longer the times of the suffocation of female desire, and even less of 'a moral condemnation and a social rejection of defenceless women who have not been able to or not known how to distance themselves from male concupiscence'.[62] According to the point of view adopted on female sexuality, the bottle is either half full or half empty, but not completely empty!

What does 'putting the brakes on the sexual drive' mean? Education and culture teach us, more or less efficiently, to sublimate it. The law tries to contain it within the limits of reciprocal responsibility. But it is difficult to change it, as many news items prove every day. The drives are never completely domesticated. Sexuality is not beholden only to individual conscience or to moral imperatives defined differently according to the era. Neither is it to be confused with citizenship. It belongs to a different world, a world of fantasy, egotism, the unconscious. That is why it is puzzling to read statements such as 'it is time for men to put their sexuality in question',[63] or to find talk of 'educating citizens into a relationship between men and women founded on equality and respect for the other and to leave behind *an archaic vision of male sexuality*'.[64] To modernize sexuality, as if it were fashion!

It is even more stupefying to read the following passage written by an abolitionist, a call for a general brainstorming.

We ask the men from the associations, political parties and trade unions to get together, to work on their sexuality and on their relationship to the system of prostitution [. . .] to come up with solutions to their instincts, desires, irrepressible needs [. . .] to envision the eradication of this violence towards women,

towards children, that the repeated, mercenar
sexual act contributes to.[65]

As if activism could put an end to the male drive, u.
and children' always had to be associated (note how adoi..
cence no longer exists and that one passes directly from child
to adult, except for prostitutes, who are never totally adult),
as if finally it was a matter of deciding what constitutes good
sexuality through the adoption of a motion taken through a
majority vote. It would be better to make a good daily dose
of bromides compulsory!

Boys like girls

It would appear that, like it or not, female sexuality is the
most commendable of the two. Not only do softness and tenderness set women apart from the violence and domination
that belongs to the archaic sexuality of men, but these are
barred to women because of their very physiology. To allevi-
ate this irreducible difference, a solution is more or less
openly proposed: bringing male sexuality closer to female
sexuality. To do this, we should raise our sons like our daughters. Christina Hoff-Sommers has clearly shown in her book
The War against Boys that the war against male stereotypes
has already started in the US.[66] It is not a question of fighting
against the excesses of masculinity but against masculinity
per se, accused of being the root of all violence. In fact, she
notes, hearing it praised has become increasingly rare. On the
contrary, all of the positive values associated with it are now
systematically denigrated. Courage and risk-taking are associated with recklessness, as contrary to the principle of
caution, strength with a violence that only causes devasta-
tion, the desire for conquest with the ultimate sin, a guilty
imperialism.

This conception of masculinity is harmful in two ways.
First of all, these characteristics traditionally attributed to
men belong in fact to both sexes. Through their denigration,
not only is the male gender deprived of them, but they are

disallowed in the other. Anyone who conceives of women only as victims in need of protection does not imagine that they can say no, give a couple of slaps, in sum, defend themselves physically and morally. The image of the silent, passive and submissive woman cannot be easily reconciled with learning self-defence in college. Then again, many 1970s and 1980s feminists have had the bad experience (in terms of their ideological prejudices) of the failure of asexual education. Not that the household chores should be separated into male and female ones. But to impose the same toys, activities and objects of identification on both little girls and little boys is absurd and dangerous. The apprenticeship of sexual identity is something vital, and even if some may not like this, it is done through opposition, caricature and stereotype. Not only should it not be an ordeal for boys,[67] it should be, on the contrary, the very condition of their later coming together with the other sex. It is only when there is no longer a question mark over the feeling of male identity that boundaries are effaced and complicity can arise.[68] The resemblance between the sexes is to be found at the end of the road and certainly not at the beginning. Education can achieve everything, said Leibniz, even teach bears to dance. But the little boy is not a bear and you do not mess with the acquisition of sexual identity.

This is why it can only be worrying to hear repeatedly that certain people wish to align male sexuality to female sexuality or to proceed to the policing of bodies. What should we think, for example, of the demand to make men urinate sitting down, like women? Women belonging to Berlin's alternative scene were not the only ones to adopt this fantasy. *Libération* reported that in 1998 'they put signs on their toilets representing a male figure urinating standing up, crossed out with a big red slash: judged to be incapable of pissing standing up without getting it all over the toilet seat, men are ordered to sit down'.[69] Same thing in Sweden, where it is good practice, in certain circles, as much hygienist as they are feminist, to teach little boys to pee sitting like a girl. As early as 1996 an angry man wrote to the paper *Göteborgspoten* to denounce these 'cruel mothers who force their little darlings to wee sitting down'. The English magazine *Sterling Times* dedicated a long article in April 2000 to this phenomenon affecting the new generation of Swedes. It points out that, among other things, a feminist group from the University of Stockholm has campaigned to have all urinals removed. To stand is considered to be the height of vulgarity and suggestive of violence; in brief it is a nasty macho gesture. For the time being, men grumble but do not really dare to resist. Many young fathers feel forced by their partner to teach their son this new, very feminine, bodily technique.

One can smile, or see in this a form of symbolic violence, certainly softer, but symmetrical to the kind reported by Samia Issa as taking place in a Palestinian refugee camp in Lebanon.[70] There, men have eliminated women's toilets on the pretext that they implied a provocation. The women are reduced to using plastic bags. In this case, it is right to speak of male domination. But in the former, would one speak of female domination?

In matters of sexuality, today's defensive feminism is at the heart of a double contradiction. Without ever speaking out on the subject of the sexual freedom of women, it preaches an ever more severe cloistering of male sexuality that ricochets on women's sexuality. The gradual extension of the notion of sex crime and the repression of these last few years are helping to draw up a blueprint for a legalized, moralizing and sacralized sexuality radically opposed to the kind of sexual freedom that the newer generations make use of (some might say abuse). On the other hand, this feminism does not exclude a differentialism that preaches the resemblance of the sexes at the very point where there is none. To fight against male *imperium* is a necessity; but the deconstruction of masculinity in order to align it to traditional femininity is a mistake, perhaps even a transgression. To change man does not mean to make him disappear. One *is* the Other, but only if One *and* the Other persist.

4
Regression

The principal goal of any kind of feminism should be to bring about the equality of the sexes and not to improve the relations between men and women. It is better not to confuse the objective and its consequences, even if sometimes people pretend that they do go together. Feminists differ on the concept of equality and the means of achieving it and this brings to light some very different points of view on the relationship between the sexes. According to various feminist groups, maintaining a complicity with men is essential, contingent or impossible.

The fact remains that any feminist discourse addresses itself first of all to a female public that couldn't care less about the ideological battles of theoreticians, even if it is women who are the first to feel their effects. However, for the majority of women, the condition of their existence could get better only if equality is achieved without endangering their relations with men. Even if they fully understand that the master cannot be deprived of his privileges without putting up some resistance or at least gnashing his teeth, they also know that Margaret Mead's saying holds true: when one sex suffers, the other one does so as well. Most women and men want to live together and to get along better, even if the former find progress too slow, and the latter the sharing of the

spoils too fast. Radical feminism has little chanc
any impact on them.

Today, the question arises of the balance sheet of thu_
inist current that has been dominant during these last fifteen
years. In step with a globalized world, this feminism sometimes insists on difference, sometimes on victimhood, sometimes on a mixture of both. Equally at ease within political
parties on the right or on the left, in European governing
bodies or within various grass-roots organizations, its credo is
made up of two main propositions: women are always the
victim of men and they demand a particular protection;
women are essentially different from men, and the equality
of sexes demands that this difference be taken into account.

These two postulates, which often cannot be separated, are
currently dominant within the whole of the European Union.
They define a model for the relationship between the sexes
and a conception of equality whose consequences we must
now take stock of. What is the current state of the relationship between men and women? Is giving pride of place once
again to biological difference useful or not for the emancipation of women?

When everyone thinks they are the victim of the other

It is useless to turn a blind eye: the relations between men and
women have hardly progressed in recent years. With increasing individualism, it is even possible that they have become
worse. Not only have the points of contention not been eliminated, but they have become even more problematic. Each
sex claims to be victim of the other, the only difference being
that women shout it from the rooftops while men whisper it.
Women talk of how tired or angry they are still to be facing
an unequal share of power and duty. Men feel they are
deprived of their specificity and that they are burdened with
quite contradictory expectations. At the very same time,
they are asked to hold on to the virtues of their grandfathers
(protective strength, courage, sense of responsibility) and to

acquire those of their grandmothers (empathy, tenderness, compassion). In short, they often experience an unpleasant feeling of identity confusion vis-à-vis women, who have fewer and fewer qualms about behaving like men used to, even to the extent of laying down the law. In the literal and the figurative sense; individually as well as socially. At the same time we must guard against generalization. Male/female relationships can differ completely according to social class and generation.[1] It is inappropriate to amalgamate the condition of women from the most deprived areas and that of women in the middle or upper classes. It is inaccurate to imply, without any proviso, that women in general are the victims of men in general. Reality is infinitely more complex, and offers both sexes reasons to claim to be the victim of the other.

It has been easy to perceive the increasing power of feminist ideology in the last fifteen years. Paradoxically, it is at the very moment when feminism develops the theme of women's victim status that it starts imposing its way of thinking on a large proportion of society and its protective laws get passed in political assemblies. Since the increase in penalties for rape, we can observe the introduction of new sexual offences (harassment, prostitution of sixteen and seventeen year olds) aimed primarily at men, and the adoption of laws favouring women (pertaining to parity or to the surname). This is not the place to discuss whether or not these changes are well founded, but to point out that feminism has a real influence in important spheres of power. These new laws have benefited from the strong support of the media, often accompanied by what amounts to a trial of the male gender, without attracting any opposition from men. If these factors are taken into account, it is hardly surprising that there is a general feeling among men that women are perhaps not such powerless victims as they claim to be.[2]

Planning the end of their (indefensible) privileged position is fine, but men are less and less tolerant of the repression of behaviour in the private sphere and especially the vague notion that their entire sex is guilty. Reading the report on masculinity published by *Elle* magazine, on the occasion of

Women's Day, it becomes obvious that there are hardly reasons to rejoice.[3]

Outside the prison of political correctness, men of all generations do not hesitate to speak of their discomfort and of the resentment they feel towards women, whom they consider to be the great beneficiaries of the last thirty years. Dispossessed, disoriented, bitter or worried, they imagine themselves in their worst nightmares as male objects, castrated, useless (even for the purpose of reproduction). The older ones talk of the 'champions' who defeated them, the younger ones of 'female domination'. All of them are wary of their new rivals.

Reading this exceptional report, it is noticeable that men often perceive themselves as the victims of changes that were imposed on them, victims, as well, of unfair accusations. They attribute to women an all-powerfulness that women do not recognize in themselves. Truth be told, feminism has won the ideological war. It finds itself today endowed with considerable moral and guilt-inducing power. But men seem to forget that they jealously preserve the power that is the condition of all the others, that is to say economic and financial power. It is useful to remind readers here that despite women being better educated than men,[4] there are more unemployed women than men; that with similar qualifications and experience, women still earn less than men; that the 'glass ceiling' is not a myth since women represent only 8 per cent of the total of directors of the 5,000 biggest French companies and make up only 5.26 per cent of the board members of the 120 biggest companies in France;[5] that many men use their financial superiority to leave most domestic and familial tasks to their female partner.

Men, as individuals, do not feel responsible for this state of things, and only speak of the moral condemnation that envelops them all.

Most men cannot relate to the criticism while it is only the question of violence and male domination that is raised. With all the attempts to impose a new sexual morality on men, the separatism that nobody wants looms closer than might be suspected.

Therefore it is no longer illegitimate to ask the following questions: has the rhetoric of victimhood not played itself out in the wrong direction? Would it not have been better to engage in hand-to-hand combat in all of those domains, private, public or professional, which are permeated by inequality?[6] In other words, would it not have been better to take to the streets in protest against these injustices rather than standing in judgement over men?

When the law of difference reigns

The feminism of today should also alert women as to how their condition has changed. Wrong-footing universalist feminism, it has got rid of the concept of equality and promoted the return of biologism at all costs. The hymn to nature has suffocated the social and cultural struggle. The picture of woman has refound its old frame and this seems to suit a lot of people.

Between the child woman (the defenceless victim) and the woman-mother (for the purposes of parity), what place can there still be for the ideal of the free woman we have dreamed of for so long? Perhaps this ideal is no longer possible within a system of thought that weaves freshly every day the idea of female nature in opposition to male 'culture'. *Woman* is prisoner of her nature, *men* are summoned to change their culture. It is a contradictory message if there ever was one. It gets the women off track and exasperates the men. It is a message that men understand and discreetly savour.

The greatest progress accomplished in these last decades has all been down to the daring deconstruction of the concept of nature. Not in order to deny that it exists, as has often been said, but in order to put it in its proper place. In this way everyone has been offered an unprecedented degree of freedom compared to the traditional roles that used to define gender. It is this culturalist and universalist philosophy that has changed the female condition and removed the opprobrium attached to homosexuality. It was finally understood that sex, gender and sexuality do not predetermine destiny. But that particular discourse is no longer in fashion. Twice in the space of ten years France has given women, but also the whole society, a strong signal that differentiation is to be promoted. Even though they appear different from one another, both cases imply, on the one hand, that women do not have the same rights and responsibilities as men, and on the other, that they form a society apart from men. The first sign was allowing the Islamic headscarf to be worn in schools; the second was the inscription of sexual difference in the Constitution to justify positive discrimination.[7] In one case, feminists forgot to protest; in the second, it was they who put biological difference on the agenda, and with it the specialization of roles.

From cultural relativism to sexual particularism

It all began in the 1970s and the 1980s with the questioning of the universality of the law. Universality was judged fallacious because under the guise of neutrality, it tended to express only the interests of the powerful. Between the Marxist critique of ideological superstructures and the denunciation of ethnocentrism by Lévi-Straussian anthropology, universality was confined to the dustbin of history. The law, emptied of its content and deprived of its legitimacy, had lost its authority.

The first to feel the heat was the Universal Declaration of the Rights of Man. Accused of being only the expression of Western culture and of Judeo-Christian values, some saw in it an imperialism to be fought in the name of respect for other cultures. Cultural relativism had entered the political scene in full force and the equality between the sexes was going to pay the price. The first offensive was on the occasion of an attempt to understand the families of migrant workers from Africa. The right to polygamy and the genital mutilation of little girls was discussed in a learned manner. Carried away by self-hatred and blindness, many called for a scrupulous respect for foreign customs. Young African women pleaded in vain that French law be applied to them, but relativist sensitive souls pretended not to hear. Not only were the new arrivals not taught for years the laws of the Republic, but a blind eye was turned to some of their practices which were absolutely contrary to those laws. The representatives of the state and of its institutions, terrified at the thought of being accused of intolerance, bowed down in front of difference, whatever the cost to the victims. Benoîte Groult and other feminists, as well as the courts, required a great deal of courage and conviction to continue the fight against intolerable tolerance. After years of guilt-inducing proclamations, the relativists abandoned this charged terrain to invest in other areas, without however showing any signs of repentance.

It was in 1989, on the occasion of a debate on the Islamic headscarf, that universalism was dealt its first big defeat, and that for the first time a difference of status between men and women was admitted to. Under the seemingly anodyne event of young Muslim girls wearing a headscarf to school, a double transgression was being occluded, one serving to hide the other. Indeed, it was not only a challenge to traditional secularism, but also an affirmation of specific duties falling on women by virtue of their nature. It is likely that the young female agitators, whether encouraged or not by their parents, never understood the significance of their act. Nobody really cared enough to explain to them that they were jeopardizing the idea of the equality of the sexes and consequently, the liberation of women within their own community. On the contrary, many hastily ignored the symbolism of submission to see in it only an act of freedom that called for indulgence, according to some, or respect, according to others.

Wearing a veil or a headscarf, as imposed by fundamentalists, means that a woman must hide her hair in order not to be an object of desire. It is the signal for all men who are not members of her family that she is unapproachable and untouchable. Without it, not only is she provocative, but she takes responsibility for this provocation and for its consequences. From the outset, woman is guilty of eliciting impure desires, while man is innocent of experiencing them. A woman's body does not have the same value as a man's. It constitutes a threat that has to be dissimulated in order to desexualize it and render it inoffensive. The headscarf of the young French schoolgirls and the burka of Afghan women have the same symbolic significance: to hide this body that men must not see lest they turn it into their object. There is only one difference: the degree of fundamentalism is obviously not the same in one society as in the other.

By allowing the Islamic headscarf to be worn in state schools, the Republic and French democracy perhaps showed their religious tolerance, but they frankly abandoned the requirement for equality of the sexes on national territory. They even gave a strong signal in an opposite direction and this was not lost on everyone: do what you want with your daughters, it is no longer our business. Curiously, the government of that time, full of relativist dogma, thought it was a good idea to give in. The silence of official feminism, pretending to think that it was much ado about nothing, was even stranger. The received wisdom was as follows: the more you protest, the more challenges to the law would multiply and this would play into the hands of the extreme right. Those against the wearing of the headscarf were asked to keep quiet so as not to be the accomplices of Le Pen. But the fashion of the headscarf, instead of disappearing as predicted, spread everywhere little by little as a rallying call or a challenge to the values of the French Republic.

The consequences of this renunciation have never been properly understood. The headscarf was only the visible tip of the iceberg. Through it a certain conception of the young girl gained legitimacy in neighbourhoods with a Muslim majority. This attitude is being challenged today by the young girls from the suburbs: 'Ni putes ni soumises [Neither a whore, nor submissive]', they say,[8] because for the last ten years these are the two images of them that have tended to dominate. Either they want to live like other French women by making use of the rights that are legitimately theirs, and then they encounter the disrespect and the violence of the boys. Or they submit to the will of the men who lock them into the family. The president of the association[9] that has launched the call for liberation, Fadela Amara, aged thirty-eight, has made this painful observation:

> The regression of the status of women in the neighbourhoods [where the feminist message has never penetrated] manifests itself by a renewal of violence against girls, forced marriages, harassment by boys. There is no talk of sex in either the families or in the neighbourhood. Smoking is not allowed. Putting on a skirt is not allowed. Hanging out with boys is not allowed, under pain of being considered the neighbourhood tart or slapper. We cannot participate in conversations, we are told to 'go home' and to 'fuck off'. Girls are taken out of school: the myth of the *beurette* who studies has been blown to bits.[10]

The deterioration of the relationship between men and women in certain areas is frightening. 'For years,' says Safia, aged twenty-eight, 'my sisters, cousins, my friends, have had to live with this violence. There is a real regression. Before [when?] we felt a real solidarity, today, we young women, we hide, we stick close to the walls.'[11] And Fadela Amara, who declares herself a practising Muslim, admits: 'In families from the Maghreb, the instruments of oppression are stronger. *Fundamentalist influences have a direct effect on boys*: they are immediately translated into violence towards their sisters, their neighbours.'[12] Words confirmed by Kahina, a master's student in economics, and sister of Sohane Benziane, burned alive by young hooligans from Vitry-sur-Seine: 'From the moment there is a doctrine that says that woman is inferior to man, then the door is open to excess. And I think that the debate on the wearing of the headscarf is ridiculous. Islam must be put on the same level as the other religions. [. . .] *The wearing of the veil should be forbidden in schools.*'[13]

Not only has the Republic abandoned those very neighbourhoods that are experiencing the greatest difficulties. By giving in to communitarian pressures, by adopting a philosophy of differentiation, it has allowed an intolerable process of women's oppression to operate in its midst. It is high time to reverse the trend and to renounce an ideology responsible for such a disaster. It is high time, as well, to be reminded that no religion, no culture, can ever have the last word against the equality of the sexes. Like it or not, this equality is best guaranteed by a universal law that everyone has to observe rather than a relativism that opens the door to all kinds of exceptions.

Feminists were convinced of this until the moment when some thought they could make the emancipation of women take a decisive turn by proclaiming a sexual particularism. It was on the occasion of the second defeat of universalism, and it was this that probably marked the undoing of women.

To justify the inscription of sexual dualism in the Constitution in 1999, certain partisans of parity performed philosophical contortions that had no other goal than of highlighting once again biological difference and its particularities. The universal was accused of being male and humanity of being an abstraction. The idea of a mixed universal and a dual humanity was invented, without any regard for the contradiction in terms. Exit a concept of humanity unifying all human beings beyond their differences of sex and race, and the notion of universal was well and truly emptied of its content. But this was not the most serious thing. The biased analysis of concepts does not signify their disappearance. In fact, the philosophy that presides over this analysis implies a conception of women and of the relationship between the sexes that has serious consequences.

Biology and the difference of roles

By making biological difference the ultimate criterion for the classification of human beings, you are condemned to think the one in opposition to the other. Two sexes, so two ways of seeing the world, two types of thinking, two types of psychology, two different universes that remain side by side without ever being integrated. The female is a world in itself, the male is another, which makes crossing borders difficult and seems to ignore social and cultural differences.

By deducing femininity from the capacity for motherhood, woman is defined by what she is and not by what she chooses to be. On the other hand, there is no symmetrical definition of man, who is still identified by what he does rather than what he is. The recourse to biology only concerns woman. Man is never defined by his capacity for fatherhood or the bulk of his muscles. She is shackled to her body, from the outset, while he is liberated from his. Motherhood is her destiny while fatherhood is his choice. This sexual configuration poses more questions than it solves. If motherhood is the essence of femininity, one is left thinking that a woman who declines it is abnormal or ill. By being labelled 'virilist', her identity is taken away, and she is said to be undeserving of her sex. It is as if she is ejected from the community of women. If the sterile woman is to be pitied, the one who declines the state of her peers is condemned for her egotism. And in this there is a clear indication that motherhood is not a choice but a necessity whose time can at most be put off, but not escaped.

Even if political correctness forbids any explicit condemnation of those women who are not mothers, it is noted at every turn that they have become alienated from themselves in order to forge ahead in a male world. So doing, not only do they betray the cause of women, but they turn their back on femino-maternal virtues. Therefore, the 3 per cent of French women who do not want to be mothers and make use of their freedom cannot be classified through the adopted criteria. Neither men nor 'real' women, they are always creatures apart who are regarded with suspicion.

Apart from these women left to their freedom, the conception of the woman-mother also leads to a theory of female psychology inscribed in nature that is far from self-evident. The capacity for motherhood is seen to unite the female gender as much through its common characteristics as through its common preoccupations. We have gone over the former when discussing the debates on parity, in which women described themselves as more altruistic, more down to earth and more peaceful than men, as if all these virtues were innate and not the result of an apprenticeship and a social conditioning. There has been a general pretence that women's common interests are greater than their divergences, to the point where women are made to constitute a political entity distinct from the other sex. Two points of view on the world: a female one and a male one. The class struggle and the differences in male interests have been forgotten a little bit too quickly. By the same token, you have to be deaf not to hear the many different female points of view, notably on the topics that primarily concern them: abortion, maternity pay, part-time work or parity.

In truth, sexual relativism as a political principle is a trap. Men and women do not constitute two separate blocs. On the one hand, one doesn't vote by virtue of one's sex, but because of one's interests and ideology. On the other hand, there is much less difference between a man and a woman of the same social and cultural status than there is between two men or two women from different spheres of life. Contrary to what we have been led to believe, sexual difference counts for little beside social difference and the unemployed mother of two does not have the same priorities as the professional *énarque* mother[14] or the company director.

Finally, what seems more serious to us are the immediate and practical implications of sexual differentialism. In making the biological the criterion setting women apart, the specialization of roles that we have tried to counter for more than thirty years is justified in advance. Under cover of the fight against horrible neutrality and abominable undifferentiation, the old male and female stereotypes are re-endowed with an unforeseen vigour. It is very much to be feared that men have everything to gain by this and women a lot to lose.

The trap

Having two opposing feminist discourses following one another in rapid succession gives rise to confusion. Women and men between thirty and forty have today inherited the

advantages of the first one without even knowing it. They
wallow in the second one without even wanting to. Women
hold dear their sexual freedom, the ideal of equality and the
sharing out of roles without taking into account that these
three demands call for a radical rupture with an old belief
system. The return of the biological over more than ten years,
unchecked by any counter-attack from feminism, makes the
march towards equality difficult if not impossible. You cannot
simultaneously invoke maternal *instinct* (instead of talking
about *love*) and hope to involve men more in the education
of their children and make them more responsible for day-to-
day household tasks. However much this is made into a moral
and psychological duty, men are simultaneously offered a
getout clause. It is striking to see how far the couplet
woman/family has been left unchallenged in the media these
last few years. The maternalist ideology has returned in full
force and motherhood has once again become the intangible
pivot of female life. And so, young women are the target of
contradictory injunctions and are split between two feminisms that cancel each other out. On the one hand, the feminism of equality ceaselessly reminds them that despite being
better at school than boys, lower salaries and the double
working day remains their lot. These two injustices have
hardly changed over the last ten years.[15] On the other hand,
the feminism of parity adjures them to safeguard their femininity, endangered by the fallacious male neutrality and to
remember that they are mothers above all.

The results are hardly scintillating.

Maternal instinct and breast-feeding

The great return of the maternal instinct is the logical consequence of the dominant ideology, naturalist and assigning
of identity. Some radical ecologists, sociobiologists, and a
number of paediatricians and psychologists preach a return to
safe values and join their voices to those of the advocates of
difference in order to convince women that they have been
misled by their feminist mothers. Nature does things well, we

are told, and mistakes are always society's doing. Maternal instinct exists and everyone takes pride in encountering it every day. People of either gender who question this concept have understood nothing about women or motherhood. By underlining the failures and difficulties this involves, they create guilt feelings in numerous mothers deprived of their points of reference and a discomfort in all those who wish to live their maternity fully. Even more seriously, if maternal instinct is particular to women, contesting the former's existence is equated with condemning the latter. To show that in certain periods of our history, generations of women have paid little attention to their progeny[16] is simply a sacrilege that simultaneously affects women's dignity and their identity.

Antoinette Fouque and Sylviane Agacinski have inscribed themselves from the outset into this problematic. The former, by making gestation and the maternal relationship into the foundation of ethics. The latter, by promoting mother love to the rank of the model for female solicitude. To quote her:

> Yet for the mother, her child, and even her unborn child, is immediately something other than an outgrowth of flesh. It is what she cares for absolutely, that towards which she feels an infinite responsibility. That is why the behaviour traditionally qualified as 'maternal', far from being an enclosure in some sort of immanence, can constitute a universal model of an opening to caring *alterity* in general.[17]

As Pascale Molinier remarks,

> From this perspective, motherhood is conceived of as a spontaneous psychological capacity, better yet, as a natural virtue whose origin is left ambiguous. On one side, S. Agacinski never goes so far as to say that maternity would be strictly pre-given by the biological event of gestation. But on the other side, as maternity reveals itself as having no other origin than its 'immediacy', what is being proposed to us is nothing other than a 'philosophical' clothing of the maternal instinct.[18]

The American sociobiologist and primatologist Sarah Blaffer Hrdy, less dogmatic than some of her colleagues, takes many precautions when she speaks of different Maternal Instincts in mammals. In fact, she puts in its proper place the recent discovery of a so-called 'gene of the maternal instinct', arrived at through the extrapolation of an experiment done with mice.[19] She readily points out that mammal mothers do not necessarily show a complete and systematic attachment to their newborn just after birth, but that their 'maternal instinct' develops progressively, in little stages that involve the baby as well. All the same, the extreme importance that is given to the hormones of maternity, to prolactin that permits the rise of the milk and to oxytocin that triggers, she says, 'a state of euphoria', authorises her to speak of an instinct, a sort of Ariadne's thread that connects mammals, from the mouse to the woman. The fact that 50 per cent of women refuse to breast-feed, and that many do not experience this state of euphoria, does not prevent her from concluding that there is a biological basis to maternal emotions. However, she is not afraid of showing some doubt and of affirming that mothers are not the only ones capable of these emotions. Fathers and other people who know nothing of the hormones of maternity can experience them as well. Why not speak simply of 'love' when she admits that 'maternal instinct' is contingent and progressive?

Even though the primatologist distinguishes between the human mother and the primate by reminding us that infanticide is quasi unknown among the latter and that the former needs society's help in mothering and raising her child, she constantly jumps from one to the other in order to conclude that 'mother nature's reward system [. . .] conditions a woman to make this child a top priority'.[20] Would it not be more accurate to observe that nature 'proposes' and that woman 'disposes' by function of her history, her desires and her personal interests? In this she is not an ape like the others.

As for the paediatrician Edwige Antier, who dispenses her advice to mothers over the radio, she does not encumber herself with the same scientific precautions as the primatologist does. The maternal instinct exists, she says, since she encounters it every day in her consulting room. So she can assert that it is of the same nature as the instinct to eat in order to survive, that 'it pushes her to act for her baby without thinking; that it is a preoccupation that all women have within them, it is part of the very essence of woman'.[21] To strengthen her argument, she relies not only on the hormones we have already discussed, but on the gene of maternal instinct in the mouse. With a little bit of imagination, you would end up thinking that woman is a mouse like any other. Of course, the sad exceptions to the rule need not cast doubt over the instinctive character of mother love any more than the anorexic's behaviour casts doubt on the natural need to eat. At least, the peremptory assertions have the merit of simplicity, even though they do not take into account the complexity of maternal feeling. On the other hand, one might well raise questions about Dr Antier's claimed objective. She says she wants to 'do away with the guilt' that women feel because of the many criticisms levelled against them. It is not certain that she will succeed in doing this by saddling them with an instinct many do not feel they possess. In truth, considerable pressure is exerted on women, moral and psychological pressure, heavy with social and economic consequences.

Little by little, the expression 'maternal instinct' has refound its status as something self-evident and its place in the current language of the media. Its validity is no longer questioned, but rather what is being asked is whether a 'paternal instinct' exists or not! It is therefore not impermissible to think that, under the cover of good intentions, the lid has been put on any counter-argument and that it has been made more difficult for today's thirty-something mothers to be mothers and to lead their own lives. Unlike women in the 1970s, they are not allowed to doubt. The dominant discourse constantly calls them back to their duties, that is to say, to their nature.

It is in the same context that the duty to breast-feed has reappeared. Instead of leaving everybody free to choose according to their wishes and their personal circumstances, there has been an unprecedented campaign in favour of mother's milk. Previously, ecologists condemned synthetic

milks; now the World Health Organization gives recommendations that become European directives, and the Leche
League takes mothers in hand. There has been the launch of

> numerous scientific works to validate the new hypothesis: the
> child who has drunk mother's milk will still derive its benefits as
> an adult. It will be better protected against ills as diverse as
> obesity, diabetes, hypertension, arteriosclerosis, stroke, asthma,
> allergies, cavities, the faulty alignment of teeth and multiple
> sclerosis. The little human would even gain a higher IQ for life,
> just by sucking.[22]

Regardless of other studies, just as scientific, completely
contradicting the first, the WHO has declared: 'Breast is
best!', and not for a mere few weeks, as is the case with the
majority of the 50 per cent of French women who breast-feed
today.[23] The experts from Geneva think that 'babies should
not touch a bottle before the age of six months, which would
also be beneficial for mothers since women who breast-feed
for a long time run less of a risk of getting breast tumours'.[24]
The word from the WHO has been translated into a
European directive about breast-feeding in March 1999.
Under the pretext of diminishing the commercial pressure to
buy baby milk, this is no longer given freely in wards, and
maternity ward staff are asked to explain to new mothers

> (a) the advantages and superiority of breast-feeding; (b) the
> nutrition of the mother and the way to prepare for breast-feeding
> and continuing with it; (c) the potential negative effects on
> breast-feeding of partial bottle-feeding; (d) the difficulty in
> replacing breast-feeding with a feed made up of baby formulas;
> (e) if necessary, the correct use of baby formulas should be
> accompanied by documentation that must not contain any
> image that might present the use of such baby formulas as the
> ideal solution.[25]

It is easy to see that a really strong will is needed in order
to resist such pressures. A woman who has given birth is
always in a weakened state. Often overwhelmed by the task
awaiting her and knowing nothing of the instinct attributed

to her, she is hungry for recommendations and ready to submit to the rules of 'professionals'. Result: some breast-feed against their will, others put an end to it soon after they return home. But what to make of the guilt they might feel at having disobeyed such powerful authorities? Fortunately, some French maternity ward staff, who have often partici-pated in feminist struggles, are more ready to respect the freedom of women than those in other countries. Thanks to this, the young French mother is less of a prisoner of the obli-gations that define motherhood than her European neigh-bours.

In fact, no feminist voice has spoken up against such regres-sive changes. There has been no media campaign to counter-balance this new way of making mothers feel guilty, something that would have been judged unacceptable twenty years ago. Many young mothers, isolated, misin-formed, abandoned, must imagine that the silence means consent.

The maternal instinct and part-time work

The combination of the economic crisis and the implicit or explicit return of the maternal instinct has had detrimental effects on the push forward to the equality of the sexes. Everything has conspired to make mothers stay at home. Payment to mothers disguised under the label 'allocation parentale d'éducation' (APE) [parental education allow-ance], equivalent to half the minimum wage, was first aimed at mothers of three children or more in 1985. Nine years later, it was extended to women who have a second child.[26] The first to choose this solution were obviously the most dis-advantaged, the less educated, those with difficult working conditions, those for whom the cost of child-care is prohibi-tive. Also, those who thought they would be better mothers by staying at home rather than spending time outside it. Many stopped working in order to benefit from this allow-ance and the results were very mixed.[27] If it was a good decision for some, others, on the contrary, were kicking

themselves. At the end of the day, many women found themselves unemployed, dependent on their partner, at times
alone and unable to return to the job market. It is they who
have born the brunt of part-time work, badly paid and with
impossible hours.[28] They were the ones who benefited the
least from the economic upturn that has taken place since
1997. They form the battalion of the employees with the
lowest salaries, and unemployment levels are at a peak among
them. Had they been offered nursery places, perhaps they
would have continued working and escaped these precarious
living conditions.

But part-time work does not only concern the most fragile
female population. Since the beginning of the 1990s, it has
been the subject of an ideological discourse aimed at all levels
of society. Presented to women, and not to men, as the
miracle solution in order to reconcile family and professional
life, it reinforces from the start the couplet women/family
and frees man from the duties he had been asked to share.
The partisans of the maternal instinct are the strongest apol-
ogists for part-time work. They even accuse feminists of
having been detrimental to mothers by slowing down the
adjustment of their working time under the pretext (which
is true) that 'part-time work would penalize women in their
income, in their pensions and in their careers'.[29] We can add
that it penalizes them as well in their independence in relation to their partner. But that is not their business, since the
priority is the conciliation between maternal instinct and
professional demands. Edwige Antier asks: 'What is preferable: to delegate your role as a mother as much as possible, or
to free yourself from a portion of your professional duties?'[30]
The answer is self-evident:

> more and more women are asking for parental leave or switch-
> ing to part-time work [. . .]. All the women I meet are ready to
> bracket off professional promotion in order to guarantee their
> children a good development. After having cradled them and fed
> them with milk and words, they accompany and support them
> during the school years. And I encourage them to do so. Because

there is time for everything in our long lives; it is possible to take up and pursue your career again when the children are grown up.[31]

Other than the fact that it is rather difficult for a woman over forty to find work, and even more to take up her career again, such an approach is manna from heaven for men who resent doing their share of parental and household tasks. 'And the father in all this? [. . .] He is fundamental', according to E. Antier. But is his role to 'change diapers, give the bottle, rock the cradle, and so be a clone of the mother', a 'new' father, something we so fervently wished he would be? Or rather 'a companion, a support for the mother, her protector, the one who glorifies her'.[32] You would think we had gone back forty years in time, even before Laurence Pernoud gave us her precious advice![33]

Is it any wonder that women with children have a shorter working day than men (an hour less per child, and nearly four and a half hours less for four children and more), but on the other hand a much longer working time at home than the father? How can one fight against the double working day of those who have full-time jobs? How can one put an end to the inequality of salaries and of roles if from the start woman is assigned an instinct that predisposes her to stay at home? If society accepts this discourse, it also justifies the specialization of tasks and with it the gap between the male and female condition. This is not what differentialist feminists want, but nothing in their discourse can prevent it from happening. You cannot at the same time separate men and women as two distinct entities with different interests, and fight for a lack of differentiation in their roles – which is nevertheless the only road to the equality of the sexes. More day nurseries, and better opportunities for child-care in the home do more for this than all the speeches on parity. Paternity leave is important as well,[34] since it symbolically marks the fact that the mother is not the only one concerned by the conciliation between private life and family life.

～

Equality is nourished by the same (=) and not by the different (≠). Misunderstand this elementary logic, force the meaning of the terms, and you end up with the opposite of what you hoped for. Parity that calls for equality in difference is a time-bomb. Very quickly, as we have seen, difference is overestimated and equality is made relative. The difference between the sexes is a fact, but it does not predestine a person to given roles and functions. There is not a male psychology and a female psychology, impermeable to each other, nor are there two sexual identities fixed in stone. Once he or she has acquired a sense of identity, every adult does what he or she wants to or is able to do. By putting an end to the omnipotence of sexual stereotypes, the path to the play of possibilities has been opened up. It is not, as has been said, the beginning of the sad reign of the monosexual. The lack of differentiation in roles does not mean the lack of differentiation in identities. On the contrary, it is the very condition for their multiplicity and for our freedom.

It is true that yesterday's stereotypes, discreetly called 'our reference points' imprisoned us but they also reassured us. Nowadays, their breakdown troubles more and more people. Many men blame the decline of their empire on this and they make women pay. Many women are tempted to answer back by instituting a new moral order that presupposes the re-establishment of borders. It is the trap we must not fall into, lest we lose our freedom, slow down the march to equality and link up with separatism.

This is the lure of the discourse that has been dominant for the last ten or fifteen years. Contrary to its expectations, it is unlikely that it will enable any progress in the condition of women. It is even to be feared that women's relations with men will deteriorate. This is what is called reaching a dead end.

The author would like to thank Micheline Amar for her precious advice.

Notes

THE TURNING POINT OF THE 1990s

1 The new reproductive technologies downplay male participation more and more, not to mention the threat to the male gender implied by therapeutic cloning.
2 Victim feminism denotes an attitude that consists in defining oneself first and foremost as a victim.
3 Antoinette Fouque, see *Marianne*, 9–15 Dec. 2002. [Unless otherwise indicated, all translations from the French are my own. Trans.]
4 *Beurette* is slang for a second generation Arab woman. From arabe = rabeux = beur(r)e (masculine) / beurette (feminine). [Trans.]
5 Which is not to be confused with the feminist discourse of Women's Studies aimed at a university audience.

CHAPTER 1 THE NEW DISCOURSE ON METHOD

1 Definition in the Robert dictionary, which goes on to say: 'Method consisting in artificially creating a whole from diverse formations, by exploiting a point in common.' The *OED*'s definition is slightly less pejorative. It defines the amalgam as 'a complete combination of various elements' and amalgamation

as 'a homogeneous union of what were previously distinct elements, societies, etc.'. [Trans.]

2 Susan Brownmiller, *Against our Will: Men, Women and Rape* (New York: Bantam, 1975). The book affirms: 'Rape is nothing more or less than a conscious process of intimidation by which *all* men keep *all* women in a state of fear' (from the cover blurb).

3 Catharine MacKinnon, *Sexual Harassment of Working Women* (New Haven: Yale University Press, 1979).

4 Andrea Dworkin, *Pornography: Men Possessing Women* (London: Women's Press, 1981).

5 Catharine MacKinnon, *Feminism Unmodified* (Cambridge, Mass.: Harvard University Press, 1987), ch. 7.

6 See Gayle Rubin, 'Thinking sex: notes for a radical theory of the politics of sexuality', in Carole Vance (ed.), *Pleasure and Danger: Exploring Female Sexuality* (Boston: Routledge and Kegan Paul, 1984).

7 An association that the lawyer Gisèle Halimi founded in 1972 to promote the cause of women. [Trans.]

8 Choisir la Cause des Femmes, *Viol, le procès d'Aix-en-Provence* (Paris: Gallimard, 1978), p. 413.

9 Georges Vigarello, *Histoire du viol, XVIe–XXe siècle* (Paris: Seuil, 1998), p. 246.

10 Article 332 of the old Penal Code.

11 In 1999, 8,700 women complained of rape and 1,200 people were sentenced. These statistics were quoted by the president of Viols Femmes Informations in *Le journal du Dimanche*, 8 Mar. 2003.

12 *Annuaire statistique de la Justice*, 1998 edn.

13 Section 3, book II of the Penal Code, emphasis added.

14 Vigarello, *Histoire du viol*, p. 254.

15 *New York Times*, 3 May 1992.

16 Loi de modernisation sociale, Article 222-33-2.

17 *Le Monde*, 19 Apr. 2002. To cap it all, European law expects the burden of proof to be the other way round. This law will take effect from July 2005.

18 L'Enquête Nationale sur les Violences envers les Femmes en France (Enveff), survey by Maryse Jaspard and team commissioned by the Ministry for Women's Rights and conducted on the telephone from March to July 2000 with a representative sample of 6,970 women. See 'Nommer et compter les violences

envers les femmes: une première enquête nationale en France',
Population et sociétés, no. 364 (Jan. 2001).

19 To have experienced more than three of these instances of psychological pressure, at least one of them frequently, amounts to the notion of moral harassment.

20 Thus, on 21 January 2003, in the course of a day devoted to domestic violence, a journalist from a local radio station announced on the 8 o'clock news: '10 per cent of French women are beaten by their husbands!' On 23 March 2003, *Libération* gave the following headline to a review of a television news magazine: 'One women in seven is beaten up in France.'

21 Interview by Marie Huret in *L'Express*, 13 May 1999.

22 *Le Monde*, 7 Mar. 2002.

23 Collectif Féministe contre le Viol, *Bulletin* (2002), p. 15.

24 Ibid., p. 29.

25 Cited by Christopher M. Finan, 'Catharine A. MacKinnon: the rise of a feminist censor, 1983–1993', at www.mediacoalition. org/reports/mackinnon.html. See also C. MacKinnon, 'Sexuality, pornography and method', *Ethics* 99 (Jan. 1989), p. 331. In 1992, the Department of Justice announced entirely different statistics: 8 per cent of American women are victims of rape or attempted rape in the course of their life.

26 Mary Koss had already published an article (with Cheryl Oros), on rape in which she maintained that 'rape represents an extreme form of behaviour, but one that is on a continuum with normal male behaviour within the culture', *Journal of Consulting and Clinical Psychology* 50, no. 3 (1982), p. 455.

27 Emphasis added. For the story of the survey and the storm it caused, cf. Richard Orton, 'Campus rape: understanding the numbers and defining the problem', *Ending Men's Violence Newsletter* (summer/autumn 1991); Katie Roiphe, *The Morning After* (London: Hamish Hamilton, 1994); Christina Hoff-Sommers, *Who Stole Feminism?* (New York: Simon and Schuster, 1994).

28 'Realities and mythologies of rape', *Society* 29 (May–June 1992). See also 'Examining the fact: advocacy research overstates the incidence of date and acquaintance rape', in Richard Gelles and Donileen Loseke (eds), *Current Controversies in Family Violence* (Newbury Park: Sage, 1993), pp. 120–32.

29 Katie Roiphe, 'The rape crisis: or is dating dangerous?', *New*

York Times Magazine, 13 June 1993; reprinted in Roiphe, *The Morning After,* pp. 51–84, at p. 52.

30 Reported by Hoff-Sommers, *Who Stole Feminism?,* p. 222.

31 *Populations et sociétés,* no. 364 (Jan. 2001, p. 4. This number of 48,000 rapes is derived from an estimate of between 32,000 and 64,000 (with a confidence level of 95 per cent).

32 Collectif Féministe contre le Viol, *Bulletin* (2002), p. 12. Let us be reminded that *Comportement sexuel des Français,* the report on the sexual behaviour of the French by A. Spira and N. Bajos (La Documentation Française, 1993), spoke in terms of 4.7 per cent of women victims of forced sexual relations, in other words a little over one in twenty (pp. 217–19).

33 *Libération,* 7 Nov. 2002; *Telécinéobs,* 2–8 Nov. 2002. Reviews of the film *Le Viol,* shown on the France 5 channel, 7 Nov. 2002.

34 Marie-Ange Le Boulaire, *Le Viol* (Paris: Flammarion, 2002), p. 239.

35 *Le Monde,* 19 Apr. 2002. We should note that Mme Diamantopoulou's numbers are still far from those advanced by MacKinnon, who affirmed that 85 per cent of American women working outside the home will have experienced sexual harassment at least once in their lives.

36 Roiphe, *The Morning After,* p. 87.

37 Except in certain works on men addressed to an academic audience, such as Daniel Welzer-Lang (ed.), *Nouvelles Approches des hommes et du masculin* (Toulouse: Presses Universitaires du Mirail, 1998).

38 Contrary to what is supposed, feminists have not waited for Pierre Bourdieu to conceptualize male domination, as Nicole-Claude Mathieu and Marie-Victoire Louis have sharply reminded us in two articles published in the same issue of *Les Temps Modernes,* no. 604 (May-June-July 1999).

39 We have not forgotten Antoinette Fouque's poisonous obituary written the day after Simone de Beauvoir's death that denounced 'her feminist positions – universalist, egalitarian, assimilating, normalizing – [. . .] this death, she said, more than an event, is an event on the historical scene, one that will perhaps accelerate the entry of women into the twenty-first century', *Libération,* 15 Apr. 1986.

40 Sylviane Agacinski, *Politiques des sexes* (1998), trans. by Lisa Walsh as *Parity of the Sexes* (New York: Columbia University Press, 2001), pp. 42 and 64.

41 *Le Point*, 1 Nov. 2002.
42 Françoise Héritier, *Masculin/Féminin I. La pensée et la différence* (Paris: Odile Jacob, 1996).
43 Françoise Héritier, *Masculin/Féminin II. Dissoudre la hiérarchie* (Paris: Odile Jacob, 2002), p. 26.
44 Héritier, *Masculin/Féminin I*, pp. 299 and 300.
45 Héritier, *Masculin/Féminin II*, p. 248.
46 When F. Héritier affirms that with the mastery of reproduction women not only change social rules *ipso facto* (by becoming fully fledged partners), but also conceptual ones (the ability to change mental categories), she qualifies her statement a little further on: 'or in any case the reversal of all category hierarchies relating to the notions that govern our systems of representation, at least a better equilibrium or a new sharing out which would ensure that a negative is not always associated with the feminine pole, nor a positive with the masculine one', *Masculin/Féminin II*, pp. 248 and 251.
47 Antoinette Fouque, *Il y a deux sexes* (Paris: Gallimard, 1995), p. 81.
48 Agacinski, *Parity of the Sexes*, p. 24.
49 François de Singly, 'Les habits neufs de la domination masculine', *Esprit* (Nov. 1993), pp. 54–64.
50 Fouque, *Il y a deux sexes*, pp. 156–7.
51 Ibid., p. 157.
52 A. Fouque also writes of gestation 'as generation, gesture, management and internal experience, experience of the intimate, but also generosity, genius of the species, acceptance of the foreign body, hospitality, openness [. . .] model of anthropoculture, matrix of the universality of humanity and the origin of ethics', ibid., p. 80.
53 Agacinski, *Parity of the Sexes*, p. 82.
54 Ibid., p. 83, emphasis in the original.
55 Ibid., p. 84.
56 Ibid., p. 109.
57 Nicole-Claude Mathieu 'Notes pour une définition sociologique des catégories de sexe' (1971), re-edited in *l'Anatomie politique, catégorisations et idéologies du sexe* (Paris: Côté-femmes, 1991); Colette Guillaumin, 'Pratique de pouvoir et idées de nature, l'appropriation des femmes', *Questions féministes*, no. 2 (1978), republished in *Sexe, race et pratique de pouvoir* (Paris: Côté-

femmes, 1992); Christine Delphy, 'L'ennemi principal', *Partisans*, nos 54–5 (July–Aug. 1970).

58 See the work of Daniel Welzer-Lang, close to Anglo-American men's studies.

59 Welzer-Lang, *Nouvelles Approches*, p. 11.

60 Ibid., pp. 111–13.

61 'Portrait de Tarek Oubrov', *Libération*, 20 Aug. 2002.

62 de Singly 'Les habits neufs de la domination masculine', p. 60. Françoise Héritier shares this point of view: 'I have alluded to all the bastions of *domains that were the preserve of men* which have fallen one after the other, even if this was in a symbolic fashion. . . . Others are already being put together again. New ones will no doubt be constructed, of a kind we cannot even imagine', *Masculin/Féminin I*, p. 301.

63 John Stoltenberg, *Refusing to Be a Man* (New York: Meridian, 1990).

64 Quoted by Welzer-Lang, *Nouvelles Approches*, p. 25.

65 Ibid., pp. 237–53. See also Michael Kimmel, 'Who's afraid of men doing feminism', in *Changing Men: New Directions in Research on Men and Masculinity* (London: Sage, 1987).

66 Emphasis added.

67 Broadcast of *Mots croisés* on the France 2 channel, 21 Jan. 2001. See the very illuminating book by the psychiatrist Paul Bensoussan, expert to the Appeal Court of Versailles, written with the lawyer Florence Rault, *La Dictature de l'émotion* (Paris: Belfond, 2002), pp. 234–8.

68 Quoted in *Le Point*, 21 June 2002.

69 Ibid.

70 Liliane Kandel, 'Les femmes sont-elles un peuple?', in M.-C. Hoock-Demarle (ed.), *Femmes, Nations et Europe* (Paris: Ceric-Paris VII, 1995), pp. 40–59.

71 L. Irigaray, *Le Temps de la différence* (1989), trans. by Karin Martin as *Thinking the Difference* (London: Athlone Press, 1994), p. 5. Cited and discussed by Kandel, 'Les femmes sont-elles un peuple?', p. 51.

72 Irigaray, *Thinking the Difference*, pp. 61–2, 63.

73 'Combat pour la libération de la femme', *L'Idiot international*, quoted in Kandel, 'Les femmes sont-elles un peuple?', p. 42.

74 The idea of parity first appeared in France in a book by Françoise Gaspard, Anne Le Gall and Claude Servan-Schreiber, *Au pouvoir citoyennes! Liberté, égalité, parité* (Paris: Seuil, 1992).

75 Cited by J. Mossuz-Lavau, *Femmes/Hommes pour la parité* (Paris: Presse de Science Po, 1998), p. 78.
76 Ibid., pp. 78–9.
77 Ibid., p. 79.
78 Elisabeth Guigou, *Être femme en politique* (Paris: Plon, 1997), pp. 28, 153, 166.
79 Ibid., p. 235.
80 *Madame Figaro*, 16 Nov. 2002.
81 Statistics for the year 2000, Observatoire National de l'Action Sociale Décentralisée (ODAS).

CHAPTER 2   OMISSIONS

1 *Violence domestique envers les femmes*, 27 Sept. 2002; see *Le Figaro*, 31 Dec. 2002 and the *Courrier de la Marche des femmes*.
2 Enveff study.
3 One understands that for those who are subjected to physical violence, or are actually locked up, leaving might be impossible.
4 According to the Enveff study, among women who admit to being victims, 10 per cent are executives, 9 per cent white collar, 8.7 per cent blue collar workers. The unemployed account for 13.7 per cent and students 12.4 per cent.
5 *Études et statistiques: Justice*, no. 19. Provisional data for the year 2000.
6 Agacinski, *Parity of the Sexes*, pp. 125–6.
7 Héritier, *Masculin/Féminin II*, p. 305.
8 Welzer-Lang, *Nouvelles Approches*, p. 23.
9 Cécile Dauphin and Arlette Farge (eds), *De la violence des femmes* (1997; Paris: Livre de Poche, 1999).
10 Marie-Elisabeth Handman deals with maternal violence in her contribution, 'L'enfer et le paradis? Violence et tyrannie douce en Grèce contemporaine [Hell and paradise? Violence and gentle tyranny in contemporary Greece]'. She rightly links it to violence in society.
11 Dauphin and Farge, *De la violence des Femmes*, pp. 35–53.
12 *Libération*, 2 Feb. 2002.
13 As yet, we do not know the role that women played in the Cambodian genocide.
14 Liliane Kandel (ed.), *Féminismes et Nazisme* (Paris: Paris VII, 1997).

15 Ibid., p. 13.
16 Ibid.
17 Ibid., pp. 14–15.
18 Helga Schubert, *Judasfrauen* (Frankfurt am Main: Luchterhand–Literaturverlag 1990).
19 Nicole Gabriel, 'Les bouches de pierre et l'oreille du tyran; des femmes et de la délation', in Kandel, *Féminismes et Nazisme*, pp. 42–54.
20 N. Gabriel observes that 'if actual participation was at one time the preserve of men, today it is no longer the case, since in Germany we see more and more acts of violence committed by young girls belonging to extreme right-wing groups', ibid., p. 51.
21 Gudrun Schwarz, 'Les Femmes SS, 1939–1945', in Kandel, *Féminismes et Nazisme*, pp. 86–95.
22 Ibid., pp. 94–5.
23 Caroline Laurent, 'Le silence des criminelles', *Elle*, 4 Nov. 2002.
24 Director of the laboratory of clinical psychology and psychopathology at the Université René-Descartes in Paris.
25 Laurent, 'Le silence des criminelles'.
26 They represent 10–15 per cent of the total who kill, humiliate and torture.
27 Article by Sophie Coignard, *Le Point*, no. 1357, 19 Sept. 1998.
28 Ibid.
29 Ibid.
30 See A. Leschied and A. Cummings, 'Adolescent female aggression', a report to the Solicitor General of Canada, May 2000, at www.psepc-spp.gc.ca. See also 'Crime statistics', *The Daily* (Ottawa), Statistics Canada, 22 July 1998.
31 Emphasis in the original, added by Fondation Canadienne de la Jeunesse.
32 *Le Monde*, 21 Mar. 2002.
33 *Le Point*, no. 1357, 19 Sept. 1998.
34 See the 1999 report by Leslie Tutty for Health Canada, 'Husband abuse: an overview in research perspectives', at www.hc-sc.gc.ca/hppb/familyviolence.
35 We can salute here the initiative of N. Ameline, the minister assigned to Parity, for creating an emergency procedure that allows for the persecuting partner to be removed, instead of the person who is persecuted having to leave the family home.

36 Sandrine Lucchini and Axel Charles-Messance, 'Hommes battus, les bleus de la honte', on *Reportage*, TV broadcast on TF1, 8 Dec. 2002.

37 Imprisoned by the stereotype of virility, husbands and lovers who are beaten by their companions do not dare to complain.

38 For example, besides those mothers who abuse their child, there are those who wrongly accuse the father of sexual abuse as a way of more effectively barring him from custody. Or there is the case of female pimps who exercise direct violence on other women. Cf. the TV broadcast on Antenne 2, special correspondent on 30 October 2002, that showed that the mafia chief responsible for the trafficking of women in the Ukraine was an elegant bourgeois woman in her forties.

CHAPTER 3   CONTRADICTION

1 Catherine Millet, *La Vie sexuelle de Catherine M.* (2001), trans. by Adriana Hunter as *The Sexual Life of Catherine M.* (London: Serpent's Tail, 2002).

2 Les Chiennes de Garde (female guard dogs), or Watch-Bitches as they call themselves in English, are a group of radical French feminists that includes leading politicians, artists and academics; for their manifesto, see their website at http://chiennesde garde.org. [Trans.]

3 In an interview given to *Nouvel Observateur*, 22–28 June 2000, the author Virginie Despentes declares without obfuscation: 'it is time that women become tormentors [of men?], including by using the greatest violence.'

4 Xavier Deleu, *Le Consensus pornographique* (Paris: Mango Documents, 2002), p. 8.

5 *Le Nouvel Ordre sexuel* is the title of a book by Christian Authier (Paris: Bartillat, 2002).

6 Notably Jean-Claude Guillebeau, Alain Finkielkraut, Pascal Bruckner, Christian Authier or Dominique Folscheid.

7 Michel Bozon, 'Sexualité et genre', in J. Laufer, C. Marry and M. Maruani (eds), *Masculin-Féminin. Question pour les sciences de l'homme* (Paris: PUF, 2001), p. 171.

8 Authier, *Le Nouvel Ordre sexuel*, ch. 1: 'Alice, Claire, Virginie and les autres'.

9 Alfred Spira and Nathalie Bajos (eds), *Les Comportements sexuels en France* (Paris: La Documentation Française, 1993).

10 The Simon report indicated that among individuals aged between twenty and forty-nine, 24 per cent of men and 16 per cent of women had experienced anal penetration at least once during their lives.

11 Janine Mossuz-Lavau, *La Vie sexuelle en France* (Paris: La Martinière, 2002), p. 29.

12 Interview with J. Mossuz-Lavau by Blandine Grosjean, *Libération*, 10 Mar. 2002.

13 Interview with J. Mossuz-Lavau by Jacqueline Rémy, *L'Express*, 28 Feb. 2002.

14 Ibid.

15 Ibid. and *Libération*, 10 Mar. 2002.

16 Deleu, *Le Consensus pornographique*, p. 117.

17 Denise Stagnara, cited in *Marianne*, 24–30 June 2002.

18 The combination of three acronyms: BD (bondage and discipline); DS (domination and submission); SM (sadism and masochism).

19 'Commerce du sexe et pratiques BDSM', in D. Welzer-Lang and Saloua Chaker (eds), *Quand le sexe travaille . . .* (Toulouse: Presses Universitaires du Mirail, Oct. 2002), p. 101.

20 'L'échangisme: une multisexualité commerciale à forte domination masculine', in special issue of *Sociétés contemporaines*, ed. Michel Bozon, nos 41–2 (2001), pp. 111–31.

21 Deleu, *Le Consensus pornographique*, p. 186.

22 Michel Houellebecq, *Atomised*, trans. Frank Wynne (London: Vintage, 2001) and *Platform*, trans. Frank Wynne (London: Vintage, 2003).

23 Dominique Folscheid, *Sexe mécanique. La crise contemporaine de la sexualité* (Paris: Table Ronde, 2002), p. 165.

24 *Elle*, 4 Nov. 2002.

25 *Le Point*, 20–27 Dec. 2002.

26 *Libération*, 12 July 2002.

27 *Le Point*, 12 July 2002.

28 Florence Trédez, 'Les bimbos de la Pop sont-elles trop hot?', *Elle*, 9 Dec. 2002.

29 The quote in the subheading above is from Philip Roth, *The Human Stain* (London: Vintage, 2002).

30 Andrea Dworkin, 'Why women must get out of men's laps', *The Herald* (Glasgow), 2 Aug. 2002, and 'Prostitution and

male supremacy', University of Michigan Law School, Oct. 1992.

31 Rhéa Jean, 'Manifeste pour l'abolition de la prostitution', at www.artifice.qc.ca/dossierarchives/72.htm; emphasis added.

32 La Meute is a varied international network of feminists, formed with the express aim of fighting degrading and sexist images of women in advertising; see their manifesto on www.lameute.fr. [Trans.]

33 Florence Montreynaud, *Bienvenue dans La Meute* (Paris: La Découverte, 2001), p. 99.

34 Evidence of Claude Boucher, director of the association Les Amis du Bus des Femmes, *Rapport sur la sécurité intérieure*, ed. Marie-Jo Zimmermann, no. 459, p. 63.

35 IFOP and EGG survey of 5 Sept. 2002, *CB News*, 30 Sept. and 6 Oct. 2002, observing that 'Power of money over feelings is no longer taboo. Love has a price, a cost and everyone awaits a return on their investment . . .'

36 Interview with Christophe Caresche, assistant mayor and socialist representative, in *Journal du Dimanche*, 29 Sept. 2002; *Libération* of 13 Jan. 2003 goes only so far as six months in prison and a 7,500 euros fine.

37 Judith Trinquet, 'La Décorporalisation dans la pratique prostitutionnelle. Un obstacle majeur à l'accès aux soins', doctoral thesis in general medicine, 2001–2. See also the excellent critical analysis by Liliane Kandel, 'Une nouvelle maladie mentale en France; la prostitution', *Pro-Choix, la Revue du droit de choisir*, no. 23 (Winter 2002), pp. 17–23.

38 N.-C. Mathieu, 'Quand céder n'est pas consentir; des déterminants matériels et psychiques de la conscience dominée des femmes', in *L'Arraisonnement des femmes. Essais en anthropologie des sexes* (Paris: École des Hautes Études en Sciences Sociales, 1985), pp. 169–245.

39 Charlene Muelenhard and Jennifer Scharg, 'Nonviolent sexual coercion', cited by Roiphe, *The Morning After*, p. 67.

40 Roiphe, *The Morning After*, p. 75.

41 Michel Feher, 'Érotisme et féminisme aux États-Unis', *Esprit* (Nov. 1993), p. 126.

42 'Le *date rape* aux États-Unis', *Enquête*, no. 5 (1997), p. 210; cited by Claude Habib, *Le Consentement amoureux* (Paris: Hachette, 1998), p. 68.

43 Patrick Hochart, 'Le plus libre et le plus doux de tous les actes',

Esprit (1997), pp. 61–76; Claude Habib, 'Les lois de l'idylle.
Amour, sexe et nature', *Esprit* (1997), pp. 77–91.

44 Feher, 'Éroticisme et féminisme aux États-Unis', p. 129.

45 Daphne Patai, *Heterophobia: Sexual Harassment and the Future of Feminism* (Lanham, ed.: Rowman and Littlefield, 1998), pp. 176–7. Loïs Pineau's essay 'Date rape: a feminist analysis' has been published in Leslie Francis (ed.), *Date Rape: Feminism, Philosophy and the Law* (Philadelphia: University of Pennsylvania Press, 1996), pp. 1–26.

46 S. Agacinski in *Libération*, 10 Mar. 2002.

47 *Bulletin national des études féminines* (Autumn–winter 2002–3), p. 123.

48 *Psychologies* (July–Aug. 1997), p. 155.

49 Bozon, 'Sexualité et genre', p. 183.

50 *Paris-Match*, 7 Nov. 2002.

51 Cited by Patai, *Heterophobia*, pp. 141–2.

52 Feher, 'Éroticisme et féminisme aux États-Unis', pp. 123–4.

53 Catharine MacKinnon, 'Sex and violence: a perspective' (1981), in MacKinnon, *Feminism Unmodified*, p. 86.

54 Ibid., p. 87.

55 Dworkin, *Pornography*, 1981, p. 53.

56 Ibid., p. 56.

57 Andrea Dworkin, *Letters from a War Zone* (Chicago: Lawrence Hill, 1993), p. 169.

58 Montreynaud, *Bienvenue dans La Meute*, p. 199.

59 Andrea Dworkin, *Right-Wing Women* (New York: Coward-McCann, 1983), ch. 3.

60 Today, it is prostitutes whom we tend to relegate to the camp of children and the mentally ill. And in this way they join the ranks of objects forbidden to male sexuality and find themselves deprived of the status of fully fledged citizens.

61 Héritier, *Masculin/Féminin II*, pp. 293–5, emphasis added.

62 Ibid, p. 295. In France this only makes sense in the case of people who have not adopted the values of French democracy and culture.

63 Jean, 'Manifeste pour l'abolition de la prostitution', p. 13.

64 Emphasis added; 'Oui, Abolitionnistes', *Le Monde*, 16 Jan. 2003, an editorial by Danielle Bousquet, Christophe Caresche and Martine Lignières-Cassou, all three MPs from the Socialist Party,

65 Editorial by Marie-Christine Aubin, *Lettre de la Commission du*

droit des femmes, Égalité Hommes/Femmes, Fédération PS de Paris, Oct. 2002.

66 Christina Hoff-Sommers, *The War against Boys: How Misguided Feminism is Harming our Young Men* (New York: Simon and Schuster, 2000).

67 See William Pollack (Harvard Medical School) and Ronald F. Levant (psychologist at Boston University), cited in ibid.

68 E. Badinter, *XY: On Masculine Identity*, trans. Lydia Davis (1992; New York: Columbia University Press, 1995).

69 Lorraine Millot, 'Les Allemandes, du combat ·féministe à l'apartheid', *Libération*, 13 Apr. 1998.

70 Samia Issa, 'Des femmes entre deux oppressions', in Henry Lelièvre (ed.), *Les Femmes, mais qu'est-ce qu'elles veulent?* (Brussels: Éditions Complexe, 2001), p. 121.

CHAPTER 4   REGRESSION

1 Report on masculinity in *Elle*, 10 Mar. 2003.

2 A feeling all the stronger today since women, who for a number of years have made up the majority of law students, have become their judges, particularly in all matters concerning the family, such as the custody of children, etc.

3 *Elle*, 10 Mar. 2003.

4 There are today 120 girls for every 100 boys in higher education, and female full-time employees in general hold better degrees than their male colleagues; see Dominique Méda, *Le Temps des femmes* (Paris: Flammarion, 2001).

5 Actiondefemme study, 'Les femmes dans les conseils d'administration des sociétés du CAC 40, du SBF 120, du premier marché des 200 premières entreprises françaises', 8 Mar. 2003.

6 On all these points, see the excellent analyses of the Groupe Marchés du Travail et Genre (Mage) led by Margaret Maruani.

7 A motion forbidding wearing obvious religious markers (including headscarves) to state schools was voted through later in 2004. [Trans.]

8 Even though they decline the label of 'feminist', because they say they do not recognize the feminism of today, all of those who have participated in La Marche des Femmes march show an allegiance to the originary feminism.

9 La Fédération Nationale des Maisons des Potes.

10 *Libération*, 31 Jan. 2003.
11 Ibid.
12 Ibid., emphasis added.
13 *Elle*, 3 Feb. 2003, emphasis added.
14 *Énarque*: a graduate of the École Nationale d'Administration, a high prestige institution. [Trans.]
15 The difference in the salaries of men and women has even, for the first time in several decades, increased slightly in 2001.
16 Elisabeth Badinter, *Mother Lover: Myth and Reality* (1980; London: Macmillan, 1981).
17 Agacinski, *Parity of the Sexes*, p. 57.
18 Pascale Molinier, *L'Énigme de la femme active. Egoïsme, sexe et compassion* (Paris: Payot, 2003), p. 92.
19 Sarah Blaffer Hrdy, in 'Mother mice lacking a particular gene fail to take care of their babies', *Mother Nature: Maternal Instincts and the Shaping of the Species* (London: Vintage, 2000), p. 148.
20 Ibid., p. 538.
21 Edwige Antier, *Éloge des mères* (Paris: Robert Laffont, 2001), p. 54.
22 Estelle Saget in *L'Express*, 31 Oct. 2002.
23 Of French mothers who breast-feed, 10 per cent still continue after three months, against 70 per cent in Sweden or Norway and 40 per cent in Germany or Spain.
24 Saget in *L'Express*, 31 Oct. 2002. She refers to the results of an epidemiological study done on 150,000 women by English researchers called the Collaborative Group on Hormonal Factors in Breast Cancer and published in the *Lancet*, 20 July 2002.
25 Official regulation published in *Journal Officiel*, 8 Aug. 1998, Article 1.
26 Decree of 1 Sept. 1994.
27 APE can also be taken part-time. Since 1994, the number of working mothers of two children has gone from 70 per cent to 55 per cent.
28 In 1998, 85 per cent of part-time jobs were filled by women and almost a third of waged women occupied these jobs.
29 Antier, *Éloge des mères*, p. 22.
30 Ibid., p. 153.
31 Ibid., p. 155.
32 Ibid., p. 20.

33 Laurence Pernoud is a prolific writer of books on mothers and babies. [Trans.]
34 Instituted in France in January 2002, paternity leave has gone from three days to two weeks. In a year, almost 300,000 fathers have taken this leave, in other words 40 per cent of men who had a child in 2002. Those who took advantage of it said that they discovered what a multiplicity of tasks fall on a new mother. See *Elle*, 30 Dec. 2002.

Index